The Let's Series of ESL

LET'S CONTINUE

The Let's Series of ESL

The Let's Series of ESL

LET'S CONTINUE

Phase Four

William Samelson

EL STREET

EDUCATIONAL

Baltimore • Washington

ELSTREET
EDUCATIONAL

An imprint of Bartleby Press
PO Box 858
Savage, MD 20763
(800) 953-9929
www.Elstreet.com

Cover Illustrations by Edward Molina
Cover Design by Ross Feldner

Library of Congress Cataloguing-in-Publication Data

Samelson, William, 1928-
  Let's continue. Phase four / William Samelson.
      pages cm. -- (The Let's Series of ESL; Phase 4)
  Includes bibliographical references and index.
  ISBN 978-0-935437-34-8 (alk. paper)
  1. English language--Textbooks for foreign speakers. 2. English language--Rhetoric--Problems, exercises, etc. I. Title.
  PE1128.S217623 2013
    428.2'4--dc23
                                                          2013029135

Printed in the United States of America

To Stephen F. White, dear friend and counselor

Contents

Preface

Phase Four: Let's Continue presents a continuation of the English as a Second Language series comprising *Phase Zero Plus: Let's Begin, Phase One: Let's Converse, Phase Two: Let's Read,* and *Phase Three: Let's Write. Let's Continue* is designed either for classroom use or for individual study with or without an instructor. The book is intended for students at the *intermediate* level of their study of English. The text presupposes an already-existing knowledge of basic grammar and verb usage. However, some chapters allow for the teaching or review of certain basic forms of grammar and syntax. It is aimed primarily at an adult college student, whether native English-speaking in need of supplementary study or a native of a foreign country wishing to advance to a higher level of English proficiency in an English-speaking environment. However, if used appropriately, the text may also be found useful for the instruction of advanced level students of high-school age.

The primary objective of *Let's Continue* is to advance the student's comprehension as well as his ability to express himself in English, both in speech and in writing. The text, therefore, undertakes to present learning situations other than those usually encountered in the classroom. For that purpose, a variety of up-to-date readings have been composed. These comprise stories, fairy tales, poems, news articles, songs (complete with music), cartoons, and graphics.

Let's Continue is designed to help students of English as a Second Language improve their ability to understand and speak, read, write, and think in English. Every selection within the text, be it of serious or humorous nature, serves to encourage student comment and interpretation. The selections are, therefore, designed to appeal to student interests and to be sufficiently meaningful to remain relevant in the days to come.

It is hoped that *Let's Continue* will enable students of English as a Second Language to extend their skills of English to greater complexity and sophistication. Though our concern here is to refine the student's usage of formal American English, primary importance is nevertheless given to extending the function of language as a means of everyday communication and expression.

Let's Continue is composed of ten chapters, each comprising ten sections. Each section fulfills a specific task of instruction, i.e., it provides a learning "core" and various practice exercises in understanding, speaking, reading, writing, and grammatical reinforcement. All of the core presentations as well as the practice exercises that follow illustrate grammatical concepts in a systematic manner.

In addition, the previous proliferation of new vocabulary is brought under control; grammatical items learned in the initial *four phases* are further examined; and new, more sophisticated grammatical structures are introduced and expounded upon in depth. Writing exercises are both more numerous and more comprehensive; dialogues take on a more sophisticated level of comprehension. The presentation of grammar here is intended to foster a wider knowledge of, and an increased competence in, the English language as a functional means of communication.

The material in each lesson is composed in a manner to render appeal to a modern and universal individual. Some of the portions should inspire further discussion; others, i.e., the dialogues, might encourage practical participation and role playing in the classroom. The ultimate aim is to expand communicative skills.

A few words about the chapter format are in order. Each of the ten sections of each chapter fulfills a specific function within the chapter. It is advisable, therefore, that an attempt be made to complete all sections. The flexibility of the presentation, however, allows the instructor or the student to select the order in which to proceed. The section approach makes it possible for the instructor or the student to determine precisely the order best suited to his needs.

Each **Model Presentation,** be it a dialogue, prose selection, poetry, song or some other form of written or oral communication, provides introductory examples for the new idiomatic and grammatical material within the chapter. Its contextual presentation is such that it will serve as the core of each lesson. Each subsequent section within the chapter is structured in reference to the core material introduced.

The **Vocabulary** section comprises words presented in the context of the Model Presentation. It serves as a means for vocabulary practice in conversation as well as written expression. The special expressions will assist students in learning the meaning and usage of phrases commonly heard in America.

The **Vocabulary Substitution** section further expands the student's knowledge of vocabulary. It allows a free association of expressions and the presentation of synonym-antonym relationships in the context of the Model Presentation. Selections comprise words taken from the Model Presentation.

The **Pictographs** of the situations comprising the Model Presentation help the students to better envision their role in its context. This makes for more active, relevant participation and for imaginative and meaningful retention of new expressions. Occasionally, songs may be presented here, both lyrics and music. They are to be sung in class. Crossword puzzles are frequently introduced to emphasize awareness of word recognition and discrimination.

The **Grammar** section presents grammatical analysis of the speech and writing items contained in the Model Presentation. Further samples are presented in varied context. An exercise section is included to serve the student in expressing varying ideas through transformation of the material learned. This type of exercise forces production and encourages the student to alternate vocabulary without changing syntactic structure.

In the **Idea Recognition** section, emphasis is placed on the recognition of logical syntactic and semantic relations within grammatically patterned sentences. The student is encouraged to develop further thought *patterns* modeled on ideas from the Model Presentation.

Included in the **Vocabulary Enrichment** section are exercises on patterns of speech, idioms, useful sayings, etc., all of which are helpful in expanding the student's vocabulary. Also, exercises in *paraphrasing* statements taken from the Model Presentation are included. The student becomes aware of alternate ways to express roughly the same idea in English. In fact, the expressions presented here are paraphrases of the original narrative; the student is to identify the paraphrased expressions in the Model Presentation.

The **Steps in Creative Expression** section helps the student learn to recreate the original Model Presentations. Given are multiple clues which the student must complete in order to achieve the goal of creating a coherent and logical unit of speech or writing. The section begins with small grammatical changes, such as "she" to "we," which in turn necessitate changes in verb structure from "goes" to "go"; then somewhat more sophisticated alterations are introduced, such as *lexical units* of structure changes, nouns to adjectives, to verbs, to adverbs, etc. As an added "vocabulary builder," a vignette describing life in the United States is included occasionally.

The **Commentary on Model Presentation** encourages students to think critically about the Model Presentation. They are asked various criticism-inducing questions which may either be answered in a straightforward manner, or elaborated on through the presentation of original compositions. These compositions are used for class recitation culminating in peer discussion and criticism.

At the point of the **Free Composition** section, the students are ready to be assigned various topics on which they will create short original presentations, imitating the forms of creative writing found in the Model Presentations. Thus, the students may be assigned to compose a short narrative or dialogue, write an essay or compose a poem, create a crossword puzzle, etc.

Acknowledgements

During the preparation of this book, I received
encouragement and suggestions, directly and indirectly,
from a great many colleagues and students, for which
I wish to express my appreciation. I also wish to thank
my colleagues who worked with this material in their
English as a Second Language classes for their
many useful criticisms and suggestions.

No acknowledgments would be complete
without giving recognition to my wife and children,
who tolerated my absence during the trying time of "labor,"
and who were first to celebrate the birth of this project.

CHAPTER ONE

How About a Game?

Physical and Mental Fitness

IN THIS CHAPTER

Words to Remember
Two-word verbs introduced in Chapter 1

become of — bring back — bring up — call up —
cheer up — come across — come along —
come over — count on — figure out — get up —
give up — go about — go on — hang up — keep on —
keep up — look out for — look forward to —
look over — make up — pay back — pick out —
pick up — put off — put on — run across —
take off — take on — take up — talk over —
throw away — try on — try out — turn off —
turn over — wake up — warm up — work up

MODEL PRESENTATION

Dialogue: How About a Game?

(Jason: J, Robert: R)

J: Hi, Robert. What's going on?
R: Nothing much. I got up this morning early enough, but somehow I can't get things going.

J: What do you say we work up an appetite with some touch football?
R: Say, Jason, now that you bring it up, I just remembered you forgot to bring back the football you borrowed quite a while ago.

J: And I just happened to remember you didn't pay me back the 10 dollars I lent you last month. You owe me some interest on it by now. I wanted to call you up to remind you. Honestly, I thought you wanted to throw away your old football.
R: Okay, okay. I give up. You can get your money plus interest when you turn over the football.

J: It's a deal. As soon as I've put on some grubby jeans, I'll come over.
R: By the way, remember to turn off on Meadow Lane before you come to the 200 block of Sapphire Street. You always get lost coming over. Sapphire is a one-way street. You can enter by way of Meadow Lane, and look out for children crossing the street.

---

go on: happen
get up: wake up
work up: create
bring up: mention
bring back: return, recall
pay back: repay
interest: profit

call up: telephone
throw away: get rid of
give up: surrender, quit
turn over: deliver
put on: get dressed
turn off: make a turn
come over: pay a visit

J: Those streets run in circles over on your side of town. It's hard to figure out which way they go: north-south or east-west.

R: Never mind that, just watch your signs and keep on going until you come to Meadow Lane.

J: By the way, did you remember to pick out a new warm-up suit for our P.E. class?

R: No, I haven't had a chance to look over some of the sweat suits that are on sale at the sporting goods store. They're having a big sale tomorrow. I'll bring it up to my father after school. Hope he has the time to take me shopping.

J: Most evenings my father's tired. All he wants to do is read the newspaper or watch T.V. Say, would your father mind picking me up at the same time? I want to try on an outfit, too. I'll come along, if he'll let me.

R: As far as I can see, he'll do it. I'll talk it over with him before we leave.

J: Hey, that's real nice of you, buddy. I'll count on it then.
    See you tomorrow.

R: So long, buddy, goodbye.

---

look out for: be careful about

figure out: reason, solve the problem

keep on: continue

pick out: select

warm up: to get warm

look over: examine

pick up: fetch

try on: test, examine

outfit: suit, dress

come along: accompany, go with

talk over: discuss

count on: depend

so long: farewell, goodbye

Narrative: Physical and Mental Fitness

"Old age is an incurable disease."
       –Seneca

1. Everybody admires the vigor of youth. Which one of us would not like to maintain a healthy vitality for as long as possible? But the older one gets, the harder it is to keep fit physically as well as mentally. Nevertheless, what becomes of us depends to a great measure on ourselves.

2. The human body requires good care. Aging comes to everyone; it is inevitable. Sooner or later, we try to slow down the aging process, but no matter how hard we try, we can do nothing to avoid growing old. As soon as we understand that, we must make up our minds how we wish to go about staying fit. Time is no longer our enemy but a trusted friend.

3. There are many ways in which a person can go about maintaining good physical and mental health. One way is to exercise regularly each day. Vigorous exercise gets the heart pumping and the sweat pouring. Exercise slows the decline of the heart and lungs. This kind of exercise builds strength, flexibility, and endurance. To build a healthy body, a person must keep up the daily conditioning.

---

incurable: fatal
admires: likes
vigor: energy, vitality
maintain: keep up, continue
vitality: vigor
becomes of: happens to
measure: degree
requires: needs
inevitable: unavoidable
sooner or later: eventually

process: steps
make up (mind): decide
go about: act, proceed
trusted: faithful
regularly: usually
pumping: pulsating
pouring: flowing
decline: aging
flexibility: elasticity, agility
keep up: continue

4. One of the most popular forms of physical conditioning is jogging. While jogging, one comes across all kinds of people: athletes who run for endurance, fat people who wish to reduce, and skinny people who want to gain weight. Some individuals run because they enjoy it.

5. While exercising, a person must consume a proper nutritional diet (low in fat and high in protein) so that the body will receive sufficient nourishment for any sustained physical effort. It is just as uncomfortable to be overweight as it is not to weigh enough. Remember, a moderate life style is desirable. The longer exercising is put off, the more difficult it will be to take off some weight.

6. In all this search for physical and mental fitness, one should look for a balance between the body and the mind. One should not take on more than the body can afford. Some types of exercises offer the opportunity for mind and body work. The most popular exercises of this kind are various forms of yoga, because they combine physical and mental activity. Yoga works on flexibility and strength as well as conditioning the entire body. Yoga is good for general stretching and excellent for breathing, relaxing, and learning to concentrate.

7. To remain healthy, many people are taking up dance in some form.

---

conditioning: exercising, getting fit
popular: common
jogging: running
come across: meet by chance
skinny: thin, lean
reduce: lose weight
enjoy: have fun
consume: eat
diet: eat special food
sufficient: enough
nourishment: food
sustained: long-lasting
overweight: too heavy
moderate: cautious, careful
put off: postpone
take off: remove, shed
fitness: good health
take on: try to do, undertake
afford: bear
combine: put together
strength: power
entire: whole
stretching: muscle expansion
take up: become involved with

Dancing offers the advantage of providing a cultural outlet while building a healthy body. Among those who practice the discipline, dancing is universally accepted as a common language. It is important to appreciate art, because art is necessary as a counterbalance in a materialistic society.

8. In conclusion, it is clear that with any type of physical and mental conditioning, a person may look forward to a longer period of useful and creative living. Now, cheer up and start with an exercise program on your way to physical and mental finess!

Dialogue Completion

Fill in the missing word in each of the blank spaces of the dialogue. Select the proper word from the words listed below. One word may be used more than once. Repeat the sentences aloud for correct pronunciation.

pay back	pick out	cheer up	count on
bring up	look over	pick up	call up
keep on	work up	try on	put on
got up	bring back	talk over	turn off
going on	give up	look out for	turn over
throw away	come over	come along	figure out

JASON: Hi, Robert. What's _____ _____ ?

ROBERT: Nothing much. I _____ _____ this morning early enough.

---

advantage: benefit
providing: affording, giving
outlet: activity
universally: generally, all over
discipline: skill

materialistic: based on things, matter; wanting more material goods
look forward to: anticipate
period: time
cheer up: be glad, happy

JASON: What do you say we _____ _____ an appetite with some touch football?

ROBERT: Say, Jason, now that you _____ _____ , I just remembered you forgot to _____ _____ the football you borrowed.

JASON: And I remember you didn't _____ me _____ quarter I lent you. I wanted to _____ you _____ to remind you. Honestly, Bob, I thought you wanted to _____ _____ your old football!

ROBERT: Okay, I _____ _____ . You can get your quarter when you _____ _____ the football.

JASON: It's a deal. As soon as I've _____ _____ some jeans, I'll _____ _____ .

ROBERT: By the way, remember to _____ _____ on Meadow Lane. And _____ _____ _____ the kids playing in the street.

JASON: I can never _____ _____ how the streets run over on your side of town.

ROBERT: Watch your signs, and _____ _____ going until you come to our street.

JASON: Hey, did you _____ _____ a new warm-up suit?

ROBERT: I haven't had a chance to _____ _____ the sweat suits at the store. I'll _____ it _____ to my father after school. He'll take me shopping.

JASON: Say, would your father mind _____ me _____
           at same time. I want to _____ _____ an outfit,
           too. I'll _____ _____ if he'll let me.

ROBERT: I guess he'll do it. I'll _____ it _____ with him
           before leaving.

JASON:.   I sure appreciate that, buddy. Can I _____
           _____ it?

ROBERT: You can. See you tomorrow.

JASON: See you.

Narrative Completion

Fill in each blank space in the text from the list of words and phrases preceding each paragraph. You may use a selection more than once and more than one word in each blank space. Read the sentences aloud.

vitality	become of	maintain	older	physically
measure	mentally	admires	harder	vigor

1. Everybody_____the _____ of youth. Which one of us
    would not like to _____ a healthy _____ for as long as
    possible? But the _____ one gets, the _____ it is to
    keep fit   as well as _____ . Nevertheless, what becomes of us
    depends to a great _____ on ourselves.

go about	as soon as	make up	sooner or later
inevitable	process	requires	slow down

2. The human body _____ good care. Aging comes to everyone;
    it is _____ . We try to _____ _____ the aging, but
    we can't avoid growing old. _____ _____ _____
    we understand that, we must _____ _____ our minds
    how we wish to _____ _____ staying fit.

decline   conditioning   flexibility   go about
endurance   pumping   regularly   keep up

3. There are many ways in which a person can _____
    _____ maintaining good health. One way is to exercise regu-
    larly each day. Exercise gets the heart _____ . Exercise slows
    the _____ of the heart and lungs. It builds strength,
    _____ , and _____ . To build a healthy body, a person
    must _____ _____ the daily _____ .

enjoy   comes across   popular
reduce   conditioning

4. One of the most _____ forms of physical _____ is jog-
    ging. While jogging, one _____ _____ all kinds of
    people. Some people want to _____ . Others run because
    they _____ it.

take off   moderate   sustained   put off
overweight   consume   nourishment   sufficient

5. While exercising, a person must _____ a proper nutritional
    diet so that the body will receive _____ nourishment for any
    _____ physical effort. It is uncomfortable to be _____ .
    Remember, a _____ life style is desirable. The longer exercis-
    ing is _____ _____ , the more difficult it will be to
    _____ _____ some weight.

strength   take on   combines   balance
entire   stretching   fitness   afford

6. In all this search for physical _____ , there must be a
    _____ between the body and the mind. One should not
    _____ _____ more that the body can _____ .
    Yoga _____ bodily and mental activity. It works on flexibility

and _____ Yoga is good for general _____ . .

discipline	outlet	practice	providing
advantage	universally	taking up	common
materialistic	necessary	important	appreciate

7. Many people are _____ _____ dance. Dancing offers the _____ of _____ a cultural _____ . Among those who _____ the _____ , dancing is _____ accepted as a _____ language. It is _____ to _____ art, because art is _____ as a counterbalance in a _____ society.

cheer up	period	look forward to	clear	type

8. In conclusion, it is _____ that with any _____ of physical and mental conditioning, a person may _____ _____ _____ a longer _____ of useful living. Now, _____ _____ start exercising!

VOCABULAR Y SUBSTITUTION

Dialogue Completion

Fill in the missing word in each of the blank spaces of the dialogue. Select the proper word or phrase from the words listed below. Read the sentences aloud for correct pronunciation. (Karen: K, Joan: J)

get dressed	quit	create	woke up	happening
profit	telephone	repay	make a turn	be careful about
return	transfer	solve the problem	mention	

K: Hello, Joan. What's _____ ?

J: Not much. I just _____ _____ . Nice of you to call.

K: Hey, let's _____ an appetite with some tennis.

J: Say, Karen, now that you _____ it, I just remembered you forgot to _____ the tennis racket you borrowed a long time ago.

K: And I remember now the dollar you didn't _____ me. You should _____ me with _____ .

J: Honestly, Karen, I wanted to _____ you about playing tennis, and here we are talking about money.

K: Okay, okay, I _____ . Hurry up.

J: I'm on my way, just as soon as I _____ _____ .

K: And remember to _____ _____ _____ on Meadow Lane. You always miss it.

J: I'll _____ _____ _____ it this time. Maybe paying attention to street signs will _____ _____ _____ .

K: Okay, Joan, see you soon.

J: See you, Karen.

Narrative Completion

Fill in the missing word in each of the blank spaces of the narrative. Select the proper word or phrase from the words listed preceding each paragraph below. Read the sentences aloud.

degree	vigor	healthy	growth
keep up	happens to	likes	

1. Everybody _____ the _____ of youth. Many people want to _____ _____ their _____ for as long as possible. We must remember that what _____ _____ us depends to a great _____ on ourselves.

faithful   proceed   unavoidable   needs
decide   steps   eventually

2. The human body _____ good care. Old age is _____ _____ . _____ , every person tries to slow down the _____ of aging, but we cannot avoid growing old. Once we understand that, we must _____ the way to _____ in staying fit. We make of time a _____ friend, not an enemy.

agility   exercising   flowing   usually
stamina   aging   act   pulsating

3. A person can _____ to maintain good physical and mental health. Vigorous exercise gets the heart _____ and the sweat _____ . One must build _____ and _____ . To build a healthy body, one must keep on _____ .

running   have fun   common
meet by chance   conditioning   lose weight

4. A popular form of _____ is _____ . When you run, you can _____ _____ _____ all kinds of peo-ple. Some people want to _____ _____ ; others just _____ _____ while exercising.

postpone   careful   food   eat special food
enough   long-lasting   too heavy   remove

5. To keep healthy, everyone must _____ _____
    _____ so that the body will receive _____ for any
    _____ _____ physical effort. It is just as uncomfort-
    able to be _____ _____ as it is to be too skinny. This is
    why no one should _____ the coditioning of the body.

muscle expansion	undertake	power	good health
whole	put together	bear	remove

6. As we search for _____ _____ ,we look for a balance
    between the body and the mind. No one can _____ more
    than the body can _____ . There are exercises which are esp-
    cially _____ _____ for mind and body work. The
    most _____ exercises of this kind are various forms of yoga,
    because they _____ _____ bodily and mental activity.
    Yoga develops _____ and conditions the _____ body.
    It is good for _____ and excellent for relaxing.

affording	practice	benefit	activity
generally	skill	want more things	

7. Some people _____ dance to keep healthy. Dancing offers the
    _____ of _____ a cultural outlet while conditioning
    the body. Dancing is _____ accepted as common language by
    people who _____ this _____ . This _____
    makes us appreciate art, and art is necessary as a counterbalance in
    a world where people _____ _____ _____ .

time	be happy	physical	anticipate

8. In conclusion, we might say that with any type of _____ and
    mental conditioning, we may _____ a longer _____ of
    useful and creative living. Now _____ _____ and start
    our exercise! You're on your way to _____ and mental fitness.

PICTOGRAPHS (WORDS IN CONTEXT)

Below are some drawings based on the dialogue presentation. Use the word(s) or phrase(s) listed under each drawing to compose your own dialogue. The same words may be used more than once. In addition to those given here, words of your own choosing may be used.

Active vocabulary: going on, get up, morning, nothing much, get things going, clock, window, sunshine, bed, pillow, dress, wash up

Active vocabulary: work up, bring up, bring back, pay back, interest, call up, throw away, give up, turn over, football, play, game, team

Active vocabulary: put on, turn off, come over, look out for, figure out, keep up, traffic, light, people, sidewalk

Active vocabulary: pick out, look over, sale, warm up, shopping, pick up, try on, outfit, count on, sporting goods, customer, merchandise

Below are some drawings based on the narrative presentation. Use the word(s) or phrase(s) listed below each drawing to construct a short narrative of your own. Words may be used repeatedly. In addition to those words listed here, words of your own choosing may be used.

Active vocabulary from paragraphs 1, 2, 3, 4: vigor, maintain, vitality, becomes of, measure, requires, inevitable, sooner or later, make up (mind), go about, regularly, pumping, decline, flexibility, conditioning, popular, jogging, running, come across, reduce, enjoy, endurance, athletes

Active vocabulary from paragraphs 5, 6, 7, 8: consume, exercising, nutritional, diet, body, sufficient, nourishment, sustained, effort, physical, overweight, moderate, put off, take off, search, fitness, balance, body and mind, take on, afford, opportunity, popular, various, combine, flexibility, strength, stretching, entire, take up, dance, healthy, advantage, providing, outlet, building, universally, common, practice, discipline, appreciate, society, look forward to, period, useful, creative, cheer up

Crossword Puzzle

The puzzle below is based on the model narrative presentation. First,
fill in the missing words in the sentences, then write them in the puzzle.

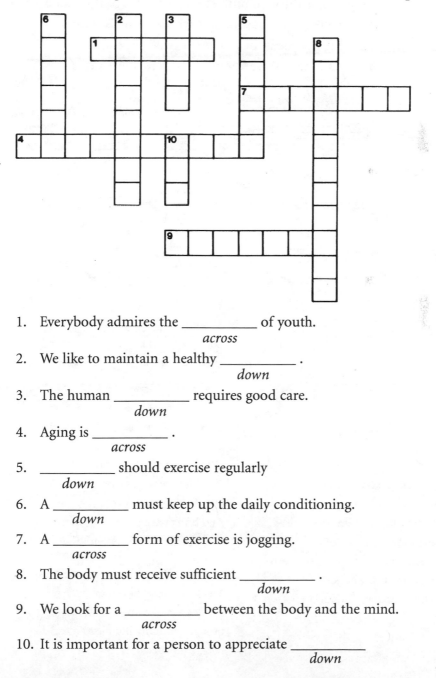

1. Everybody admires the _____ of youth.
   across

2. We like to maintain a healthy _____ .
   down

3. The human _____ requires good care.
   down

4. Aging is _____ .
   across

5. _____ should exercise regularly
   down

6. A _____ must keep up the daily conditioning.
   down

7. A _____ form of exercise is jogging.
   across

8. The body must receive sufficient _____ .
   down

9. We look for a _____ between the body and the mind.
   across

10. It is important for a person to appreciate _____
    down

Song

Below are the words and music of an old **folk song.** A folk song is a song which comes to us through much time and deep traditional background. This song tells us about someone whose name is Bonnie. We don't know who this Bonnie is, but we don't really care to know. Let us think that Bonnie is someone we know whose return we anticipate.

My Bonnie Lies Over The Ocean

Special arrangement by Rosa Samelson

Last night as I lay on my pillow.
Last night as I lay on my bed,
Last night as I lay on my pillow,
I dreamt that my Bonnie was dead.
Bring back, bring back,
Oh bring back my Bonnie to me, to me.
Bring back, bring back.
Oh bring back my Bonnie to me.

Oh blow ye winds over the ocean,
And blow ye winds over the sea,
Oh blow ye winds over the ocean,
And bring back my Bonnie to me.
Bring back, bring back, etc.

The winds have blown over the ocean,
The winds have blown over the sea, The winds have blown over the ocean, And brought back my Bonnie to me. Bring back, bring back, etc.

GRAMMAR

Explanation and Examples

Two-word verbs are frequently used in modern American English. They are usually composed of a verb plus a preposition. Two-word verbs serve as an expansion of our vocabularly. The two-word verbs are often used as idiomatic expressions.

When a verb and a preposition are used together, they have a single meaning which is different from that of the two words when they are used separately. Even though two-word verbs are often used in the English language, they are not included in commonly used dictionaries, and their idiomatic meaning must be learned in context.* We will discuss here only those two-word verbs which are used in Chapter 1. They will be presented in the context of the model presentations. For a more complete listing of two-word verbs, see **Appendix I.**

become: **become of**-happen to
What **becomes of** us depends to a great measure on ourselves.

bring: **bring back**-return, recall
You forgot to **bring back** the football.
bring up-mention
Say, Jason, now that you **bring** it **up,** I just remembered you forgot to return my football.

call: **call up**-telephone
I wanted to **call** you **up** to remind you.

cheer: **cheer up**-be glad, happy
Now, **cheer up** and start with an exercise program.

come: **come across**-meet by chance
       You **come across** all kinds of people.
       come along-accompany, go with
       I'll **come along,** if he'll let me.
       come over-pay a visit
       You always get lost **coming over.**

count: **count on**-depend on
        I'll **count on** it then. See you tomorrow.

figure: **figure out**-reason, solve the problem
         It's hard to **figure out** which way they go.

get: **get up**-wake up
      I **got up** early this morning.

give: **give up**-surrender
       Okay, okay, **I give up.**

go: **go about**-act, proceed
     We must decide how we wish to **go about** staying fit.
     go on-happen
     Hi, Robert. What's **going on?**

hang: **hang up**-put on (a receptacle, hanger)
       Don't **hang up** on me, Robert!

keep: **keep up**-continue
       Just watch your signs and **keep up** the good work.

look: **look forward to**-anticipate
       With any type of physical and mental conditioning, a

---

*Look for the two-word verbs in the following: Harold C. Whitford and Robert J. Dixson, *Handbook of American Idioms and Idiomatic Usage* (New York: Regents Publishing Co., 1973); and Thomas Crowell, *Index to Modern English* (New York: McGraw-Hill Book Co., 1964).

person may **look forward to** a longer period of useful and creative living.
look out for-be careful about
When you enter Meadlow Lane, **look out for** children crossing the street.
look over-examine
I haven't had a chance to **look over** some of the sweat suits on sale.

make: **make up** (mind)-decide
We must **make up** our minds how we wish to stay fit.

pay: **pay back**-repay
You didn't **pay** me **back** the quarter I lent you last month.

pick: **pick out**-select
Did you **pick out** a new warm-up suit?
pick up-fetch
Why don't you **pick** me **up** on your way?

put: **put off**-postpone
The longer you **put off** exercising, the more difficult it will be to take off some weight.
put on (clothing)-get dressed
As soon as I've **put on** some grubby jeans, I'll come over.

run: **run across**-meet, find by chance
At the store, I **ran across** the most beautiful running shoes!

take: **take off**-remove, shed
With exercise and proper dieting, you can **take off** some weight.
take on-try to do, undertake
A person should not **take on** more than the body can afford.
take up-practice
Many people are **taking up** dance to keep healthy.

talk: **talk over**-discuss
I'll **talk** it **over** with my mother before we leave.

throw: **throw away**-get rid of
Really, I thought you wanted to **throw away** your old football.

try: **try on**-test, examine
I want to **try on** an outfit, too.

turn: **turn** off-make a turn
By the way, remember to **turn off** on Meadow Lane.
turn over-transfer
You can get your quarter when you **turn over** the football.

wake: **wake up**-get up
I wake up early every morning.

warm: **warm up**-to get warm
Before rigorous exercise, it is wise to **warm up.**

work: **work up**-create
Let's **work up** a good appetite with a long-distance run.

Confusion will arise on occasions when the two-word verbs or verb plus adverb expressions are formed with the same verb. Verbs such as *bring, call, come, give, make, put, run, take, turn* can change meaning when combined with different adverbials. For instance, we can say

Robert *got up* early this morning.

but

Jason *got* Robert *up* early this morning.
(Jason woke Robert *up* early this morning.)

or

Jason *got back* in time for supper.

but

>Jason tried to *get* his football *back.*
>(Jason tried to recover his football.)

There are innumerable combinations of the verb *get* plus adverb, and they further change in their meaning depending on whether they are used as *separable* or *inseparable* verbs.

Examples: He *got* the package *off in* time for the holidays.
(He sent it in time for the holidays.)

or

>Jason had to *get off the* train in Austin.

>The coat was so small, he couldn't *get* it *on.*
>(He couldn't put on the coat.)

or

>It was late, and Akira tried to *get on* with his homework.
>(He tried to do his homework.)

Practice

Rewrite the sentences below. Use two-word verbs in place of the words in bold type. Read the sentences aloud.

1. Please, **return** my football.

   _____

2. Say, I forgot to **mention** it, but you owe me a quarter.

   _____

3. **Be glad,** Jason, it isn't as bad as all that!

   _____

4. When you go shopping, I want to **go with** you.

_____

5. You can **depend on** it, my friend.

_____

6. It's difficult to **reason** which way they go.

_____

7. The thief **surrenders** to the police.

_____

8. I'll **telephone** you tomorrow evening.

_____

9. Hi, Robert, what's **happening?**

_____

10. Tomorrow we'll **continue** talking.

_____

11. With proper exercise, we **anticipate** a long and healthy life.

_____

12. We have to **be careful about** children crossing the street.

_____

13. I'm going to **examine** some of the suits.

_____

14. They can never **decide** how they want to stay fit.

_____

15. His friend will **repay** him tomorrow.

_____

16. You may **select** the right exercise for yourself.

_____

17. The longer you **postpone** exercising, the more difficult it will be to start with the program.

_____

18. I'll **get dressed** in an hour from now.

_____

19. A person exercises to **remove** some weight.

_____

20. One cannot **undertake** more than the body can afford.

_____

21. To develop good concentration, they **practice** yoga.

_____

22. We **discuss** various topics in class.

_____

23. I never **get rid** of my old clothing.

_____

24. You must **make a turn** at the next corner.

_____

25. Let him **get up** as early as possible.

_____

26. Let's **create** a terrific appetite!

_____

IDEA RECOGNITION

Copy from the model narrative the sentences expressing the following:

1. What is incurable

   _____

2. What everybody admires

   _____

3. How long we would like to maintain a healthy vitality

   _____

4. What becomes more difficult to keep the older one gets

   _____

5. What depends on ourselves

   _____

6. Who requires good care

   _____

7. What comes to all of us

   _____

8. What we try to slow down

   _____

9. When we must make up our minds

   _____

10. Who becomes our trusted friend

    _____

11. What we must do regularly

    _____

12. What vigorous exercise does for your heart

_____

13. What vigorous exercise slows

_____

14. How to build a healthy body

_____

15. Which is one of the most popular forms of conditioning

_____

16. Who we run across while jogging

_____

17. Why some individuals run

_____

18. Why a person must consume a proper diet

_____

19. What is uncomfortable

_____

20. What happens when you put off exercising

_____

21. Which is the most popular exercise

_____

22. What yoga works on

_____

23. Why many people are taking up dance

_____

24. By whom dancing is universally accepted

_____

25. Why it is important to appreciate art

_____

26. How a person may look forward to a longer and more useful life

_____

VOCABULARY ENRICHMENT

Paraphrasing

Paraphrasing means rephrasing expressions or words without changing their meaning. The following are **paraphrases** of expressions or words from the model narrative. Find those expressions and write them on the blank lines below. Repeat aloud.

Example: Age can be fatal: **Age is an incurable disease**

1. a. Vigor is admired _____

    _____

    b. Everyone would like to remain young _____

    _____

    c. It's hard to maintain good health_____

    _____

    d. We are responsible for ourselves _____

    _____

2. a. The first step is understanding what is needed _____

    _____

    b. There is no need to worry about time _____

    _____

3. a. One must develop habits _____

      _____

   b. Circulation comes with vigorous exercise _____

      _____

   c. The heart and lungs become better developed_____

      _____

   d. You become stronger, more flexible _____

      _____

   e. Exercise is a daily activity_____

      _____

4. a. You run into different types of people _____

      _____

   b. Many people run for enjoyment _____

      _____

5. a. When exercising, you must eat well _____

      _____

   b. It is not good to be either too skinny or too fat _____

      _____

   c. Waiting too long will make it more difficult to start exercising

      _____

6. a. A person tries to stay fit _____

      _____

   b. A person should not overdo_____

      _____

   c. Yoga gives a balanced exercise _____

      _____

7. a. Dancing is good exercise _____
   _____

   b. Dancing offers additional benefits _____
   _____

   c. Dancers understand each other _____
   _____

   d. Art is useful in a materialistic society _____
   _____

8. a. A person's usefulness may be prolonged _____
   _____

   b. Let's get started with some activity _____
   _____

Lexical Units

Select the word (or phrase) from the words listed below that best completes each of the sentences. One selection may be used more than once. Read aloud.

Example: Everyone **grows old.**
            Old age comes to everyone.

regularly	decline	vitality	admire
popular	conditioning	make up	keep up
moderate	consume	reduce	process
take on	take up	fitness	combines
outlet	discipline	period	advantage

1. It is important to eat properly. A person must _____ sufficient nourishment.

2. The dance does not serve only as a physical exercise. It offers a cultural _____ .

3. Everybody admires the vigor of youth. We want to _____ a healthy vitality for as long as possible.

4. We want to slow down the aging process. We must _____ our minds in what way to go about achieving _____ .

5. If we wish to stay fit, we must exercise _____ .

6. Some people are overweight. They want to _____ .

7. Many people search for peace of mind. They _____ yoga because it _____ physical and mental exercise.

8. The dance offers a cultural outlet. That's why it is _____ .

9. In all our activities we should be very careful. A _____ person does not _____ more than the body can afford.

10. To achieve one's goals of mental and physical fitness is difficult. The _____ of _____ takes a long _____ of time.

Special Expressions

Below are some additional two-word verbs unlike those used in the model presentations. They are used in different contexts. Practice the sentences. Then compose one additional sentence for each new verb, using the verb in a context not previously expressed.

Example: **back up**-reinforce, support, drive or go backwards
         The second team **backs up** the varsity. = sample sentence.
         Henry **backed up** the car into his garage. = your sentence.

break down — analyze; collapse; cry; separate into parts; fail to perform or operate
When Bob heard the bad news, he **broke down** and cried.

---

bring up — introduce a piece of information; rear a family
Mr. and Mrs. Jones know how to **bring up** their children.

---

call on — to visit, come to see someone; appeal to, request something
Any time you need me, **call on** me.

---

call out — to shout, speak loudly; summon
They **called out** my friend's name.

---

cool it — keep calm, don't get excited; stop talking about it
Enough said about that! **Cool it**, my friend!

---

fall in love — become enamored or infatuated
Jim **fell in love** with the girl across the street.

---

figure out — reason; discover; solve; determine
He **figured** it **out** all by himself.

---

get along — manage; do well; leave; agree with; be friendly
Webster **gets along** with all his friends.

---

get on — put on (clothing); continue, proceed; go into; board
Get on your clothing, it's time to go!

---

hold on — wait; grasp; persevere; continue to defend
He is exhausted. He can't **hold on** much longer.

---

hold up — rob; delay
You're **holding up** progress.

---

keep up — continue; support; maintain
We must **keep up** the good work.

---

make out — write, fill out; do, fare; understand, decipher
His writing is illegible. I can't **make** it **out.**

---

make up — put together, compose; arrange, set up; imagine, invent; apply cosmetics; become friendly after a fight
Regina **made up** with her friend.

---

pick up — obtain, acquire; take up; lift; learn quickly; improve; travel faster
I've got to **pick up** a book at the library.

---

play (it) safe — be careful or cautious, don't take risks
He plays it safe whenever he makes important decisions.

---

run down — in poor health, sick; drive over; ruined or in need of repairs
The old house is very **run down.**

---

stay (stick) around — remain, stay, wait; keep close
This is a nice place. Let's **stick around** for a while.

---

take down — record, write; lower, pull down
His secretary **took down** the entire conversation.

---

take off — leave quickly; launch (rocket)
The rocket **took off** for the stars.

---

talk over — discuss; consider
We'll **talk** it **over** at our next meeting.

---

tell apart — recognize; distinguish (between)
No one can **tell** the Smothers twins **apart.**

---

turn over — overturn; deliver; give
The car **turned over** suddenly.

---

wait on — attend or serve someone
The waiter **waits on** the restaurant customers.

---

work out — solve; develop; end up, turn out
At the end, things **work out** for the best.

_____

zero in — locate accurately; adjust the accuracy of a weapon
The enemy **zeroed in** on our position.

_____

STEPS IN CREATIVE EXPRESSION

Write the two-word verbs on the line. Read the sentences aloud.

1. Hi, Robert. What's going on? _____*going on*_____

2. I got up early this morning. _____

3. Let's work up an appetite. _____

4. Why don't you bring back my ball? _____

5. I'll pay you back as soon as I can. _____

6. He wanted to call you up last night. _____

7. Don't throw away my letter! _____

8. We played better, but they didn't give up. _____

9. You never know where to turn off. _____

10. Remember to look out for children. _____

Add new words and revise the sentences, if necessary, to suit the changes indicated in parentheses. Read the sentences aloud.

Example: **Everybody** admires the vigor of youth. (We)
          We admire the vigor of youth.

1. **We** would like to maintain a healthy vitality. (She)

_____

2. What becomes of **us** depends on **ourselves.** (you, yourself)

_____

3. **The human** body requires good care. (Our)

_____

4. **We** try to slow down the aging process. (He)

_____

5. We **make up our minds** how to stay fit. (decide)

_____

6. One way is to exercise **regularly** each day. (steadily)

_____

7. Exercise keeps your heart **pumping.** (pulsating)

_____

8. Exercise slows the **decline** of the heart and lungs. (aging)

_____

9. The body must receive **sufficient** nourishment. (enough)

_____

10. The longer you wait, the more difficult it is to **take off** weight. (remove)

_____

Substitute two-word verbs for the **boldface** words.

1. Let's **create** an appetite, Jason.

   _____

2. You forgot to **repay** me.

   _____

3. Didn't I **telephone** you yesterday?

   _____

4. And you didn't **return** the football.

   _____

5. Okay, I **surrender.**

   _____

6. **Be careful** about children playing in the street.

   _____

7. **Continue** down Meadow Lane, then turn left.

   _____

8. I'd love to **select** a new shirt for my brother.

   _____

9. We'll **examine** them together.

   _____

10. You can **depend** on me!

   _____

Create a dialogue similar to the model presentation based on the expressions below. (Kevin: K, Mary: M)

K: _____ going on?

M: Not much. _____ some tennis?

K: _____ time. Will _____ come over _____ ?

M: Don't know _____ perhaps tomorrow.

K: Sure would _____ to play _____ .

M: I'll put on _____ .

K: Don't forget to _____ .

M: Yes, I know. And look out for _____ .

K: I hope you find _____ .

M: Don't worry. See you _____ .

COMMENTARY ON MODEL PRESENTATION

Using key words and phrases from the model presentation, comment on the topics presented below.

everybody	honest	overweight
admires	regularly	fitness
vigor	decline	strength
maintain	conditioning	practice
measure	popular	advantage
needs	reduce	outlet
inevitable	enjoy	discipline
sooner or later	consume	look forward to
make up	diet	period
go about	nourishment	

1. a. Discuss some ways to stay fit.

   b. Tell what you know about dieting.

   c. Express your views about aging.

   d. Write about the practice of yoga.

   e. Tell what one can look forward to when exercising.

2. a. Discuss the points in the model narrative that impressed you the most.

   b. Discuss the points in the model narrative that impressed you the least.

   c. Give an appropriate title to your composition.

FREE COMPOSITION

Dialogue improvisation: compose your own dialogue, using the situation given below.

1. It is early in the morning

2. A friend calls you up

3. You are late getting up

4. Your friend wants to play ball

5. You don't really feel like playing

6. Your friend is insistent

7. You agree to play

8. Your friend indicates the place to meet

9. You promise to come soon

10. Both of you express words at parting.

Fill in the Missing Dialogue

For each of the drawings below, write your own dialogue which describes the action.

Compose a short narrative, building on the expressions given below.

1   . . . . vigor of youth. . . . the older one gets. . . what becomes of us . . . .
2.   . . . requires. . . care. . . to slow down . . . no matter how. . . . as soon as. . . .
3.   there are . . . to exercise regularly. . . . this kind of exercise. . . .
     to build a healthy body. . . .
4.   . . . most popular. . . . while jogging . . . wish to reduce. . . .
     some individuals. . . .

CHAPTER TWO

At the Dentist's

Our Environment

IN THIS CHAPTER

Words to Remember
Two-word verbs continued in Chapter 2

abstain from — account for — accuse of — adapt to — agree on — agree with — alert against — apologize for — approve of — argue with — arrive at — arrive in — ask about — ask for — assure of — believe in — belong to — beware of — blame for — buy at — care for — caution against — complain about — contribute to — count on — depend on — die from — die of — disagree with — entrust to — fall in love with — guard against — hear of (about) — hope for — insist on — know about — laugh at — listen to — look at — look like — pay for — recover from — refrain from — rely on — result from — sympathize with — trust in — wait for — wish for

MODEL PRESENTATION

Dialogue: At the Dentist's

(Dentist = D, Patient = P, Receptionist = R)

P: I have a terrible toothache. My appointment is later in the afternoon. Do you think the doctor can see me now?

R: Ordinarily, we wouldn't be able to take you earlier. But we have had a cancellation. He should be able to see you within the hour. While you're waiting, let me ask you a few questions. Has Dr. Greene seen you before?

P: No, I'm new in the city. I asked about a good dentist when my toothache started. I complained about it to my apartment manager.

R: Did he recommend us to you?

P: Dr. Greene comes highly recommended. My apartment manager told me I can count on him.

R: Have you heard of any other dentists?

P: No, I just asked for Dr. Greene's address, and here I am.

R: Very well, Mr. Garza. Here, take these pills to relieve the pain. The doctor will be able to see you in about one hour. Can you wait for treatment that long?

P: I'll be all right. In fact, I feel better already. Thanks.

D: Well, well, young man, it looks like we're having trouble. I'm Dr.

---

receptionist: receives patients and gives information

ache: pain, hurt

ordinarily: usually

cancellation: change of appointment date

ask about: inquire

complain about: express discontent with, fret

count on: depend on, rely on

hear of: know about (the existence of) someone or something

ask for: request

wait for: delay, expect

look like: seem

presume: think

look at: inspect

cavity: hole

abstain from: stay away from

account for: explain

Greene. You're Mr. Garza, I presume?

P: That's me. Nice meeting you, doctor. I was in pain before, but I'm feeling better now.

D: That's what usually happens. Now, let's have a look at the bad tooth. Open your mouth wide! Aha . . . aha . . . just as I thought. Okay, you may relax now.

P: Is it very bad?

D: There are some cavities. Nothing serious, but you'll have to abstain from sweets, Mr. Garza. And you'll need to brush your teeth regularly.

P: How do you account for the many cavities, doctor?

D: They result from eating too many sweets. You'll have to refrain also from chewing anything that contains sugar.

P: But doctor, I love to chew gum!

D: I sympathize with you, but you'll just have to do without it. I want to caution you against some harmful foods, or you'll pay for it dearly. You have a choice: keep good teeth or go on eating sweets!

P: I'll do whatever you say, doctor. I'm not trying to disagree with you.

D: (to Nurse) Nurse, get some X rays of our patient's molars. Then we'll start drilling.

P: Drilling?

D: You have your poor eating habits to blame for this. Anyway, we'll drill one tooth at a time. No need to worry. It won't be painful with the local anesthetic.

P: I don't wish to argue that point with you, doctor.

---

result from: be a consequence of

refrain from: abstain from

contain: consist of, hold

sympathize: feel for (someone), commiserate with

caution against: warn

harmful: hurtful

pay for: give in return

choice: option

disagree with: be contrary with, argue with

molar: tooth in the back of the mouth

blame for: hold responsible for, condemn

local anesthetic: a drug to reduce pain or feeling

argue with : disagree with, be contrary with

Narrative: Our Environment

1. Probably the most important element in nature is the air we breathe. Air exists as a mixture of gases which surround the earth. Plants and animals, as well as people, breathe this precious air to live. People cannot survive without air.

2. Our environment is the place in which all of us live. We must keep our environment clean. Because we live in a mechanized world, it is difficult to keep the air clean. It is especially hard to maintain a clean environment in large cities. We must guard against making our environment unhealthy to live in.

3. When we make our air dirty and unsafe for breathing, we refer to it as "environmental pollution." Probably the one thing that contributes the most to environmental pollution is the automobile. It is true that we need the car to move from place to place, but we must beware of misusing this popular means of transportation. We need our air more than we need the automobile.

---

element: substance, material
breathe: inhale
surround: encircle
precious: valuable
survive: go on living
environment: surroundings
mechanized: automated
maintain: keep

guard against: be watchful, foresee and prevent
unsafe: not safe, dangerous
refer to: call
contribute to: be responsible for
beware of: be watchful
misuse: abuse, use badly
means: way

4. If people allow their environment to become unsafe for all life on earth, they will have no one but themselves to blame for it. The air belongs to all living things in nature, yet people are the ones who do the greatest harm to it. And although people argue with one another on many issues, they must agree on one: all life depends on clean air.

5. Therefore, all of us must make a special effort to keep our environment clean. How can we do it? We can rely on our legs more as a means of transportation. We can caution our friends against using the automobile too often. We can plant all kinds of trees and plants which produce oxygen and help keep our air pure. We can call this activity "falling in love with nature."

6. When we become aware of the great importance our environment has for us, we can always ask about how we can improve it. People cannot just wait and wish for the environment to maintain itself in spite of their efforts to destroy it. They must do their share to help keep the air as clean as nature intended it to remain. Do your best!

---

allow: permit
harm: damage, destruction
issue: topic
depend on: rely on, count on
effort: attempt
rely on: depend on, count on
pure: clean
fall in love with: become enamored of

be aware of: recognize
improve: make better
in spite of: contrary to
wish for: want
share: part
intend to: mean to
remain: stay

VOCABULARY

Dialogue Completion

Fill in the missing word in each of the blank spaces in the dialogue. Select the proper word from the words listed below. One word may be used more than once. Repeat aloud for correct pronunciation.

disagree	contains	refrain	contribute
choice	result	mouth	abstain
account	count	complained	terrible
cavity	asked	hear	saved

MR. GARZA: I have a _____ toothache. Can the tooth be _____ ?

DR. GREENE: Let's have a look at it. Open your _____ wide. Well, it doesn't look too bad.

MR. GARZA: That's wonderful. I was quite worried about it. Last night it hurt and I _____ about it to my friend.

DR. GREENE: How did you _____ of this office?

MR. GARZA: I _____ for a good dentist. My friend told me I can _____ on you, Dr. Greene.

DR. GREENE: After I fill the _____ you'll have to _____ from eating all kinds of sweets. Sweets _____ to tooth decay.

MR. GARZA: But, how do you _____ for the many cavities, doctor?

DR. GREENE: They _____ from eating too many sweets. You'll have to _____ from chewing anything that _____ sugar.

MR. GARZA: But doctor, I love to chew gum!

DR. GREENE: You have a _____ : keep good teeth or go on eating sweets!

MR. GARZA: I'll do whatever you say, doctor. I'm not trying to _____ with you.

DR. GREENE: That's better. Relax now.

Narrative Completion

Fill in each blank space in the text from the list of words and phrases preceding each paragraph. A selection may be used more than once, and more than one word may be used in one blank space.

survive	surrounds	element
breathe	precious	earth

1. Probably the most important _____ in nature is the air we _____ . Air _____ the earth. Everything that lives on _____ inhales this _____ air. We cannot _____ without air.

guard	air	live
maintain	mechanized	environment

2. Our _____ is the place in which all of us _____ . We must keep our _____ clean. Because we live in a _____ world, it is difficult to keep the _____ clean. It is especially hard to a clean environment in large cities. We must _____ against making our _____ unhealthy to live in.

means	automobile	refer
beware	contributes	unsafe

3. When we make our air dirty and _____ for breathing, we
    _____ to it as "environmental pollution." Probably the one
    thing that _____ the most to unclean air is the _____ .
    We must _____ of misusing this popular _____ of trans-
    portation. We need our air more than we need the _____ .

depends   argue   belongs   life
issues   nature   blame   allow

4. If people _____ their environment to become unsafe for
    all _____ on earth, they will have no one but themselves
    to _____ for it. The air _____ to all living things in
    _____ . Although people _____ with one another
    on many _____ , they agree on one: all life _____
    on clean air.

pure   using   rely
plant   transportation special

5. All of us must make a _____ effort to keep the air clean. We
    must _____ on our legs as means of _____ . We can
    caution our friends against _____ the automobile too often.
    We can _____ all kinds of trees and plants. They will help to
    keep the air _____ .

intended   wait   ask   share
wish   improve   aware

6. When we are _____ of the environment around us, we
    can always _____ about how we can _____ it. People
    cannot just _____ and _____ for the environment to
    maintain itself. People must do their _____ to help keep it
    as clean as nature _____ it to remain.

VOCABULAR Y SUBSTITUTION

Dialogue Completion

Fill in the missing word in each of the blank spaces of the dialogue.
Select the proper word from the words listed below. Read aloud.
(Barry = B, Sonia = S)

delay	depend	fret	know
request	inquire	pain	matter

B: Hello, Sonia. What's the _____ ? You look tired.

S: I didn't sleep all night. Had a terrible _____ in my tooth.

B: Don't _____ about it. You had better _____ about a good dentist.

S: You can _____ on that. I'm not going through another night like that!

B: I _____ of a good dentist at the new mall.

S: I'll call and _____ an appointment.

B: It's about time! You should not _____ treatment this long!

B. Repeat the following special expressions aloud.

1. I have
   — a toothache.
   — a headache.
   — a stomachache.
   — a backache

2. She has
   — a sore throat.
   — a pain in her leg
   — a pain in her shoulder.
   — a pain in her arm.

3. My
— shoulder hurts.
— leg hurts.
— tooth hurts.
— ear hurts.
— arm hurts.

4. I'm
— not feeling well.
— coughing and sneezing
— feeling a little faint.

5. I have a pain in my elbow.
He _____ a pain in _____ elbow.
She _____ a pain in _____ elbow.

6. I have a pain in
— my leg.
— my knee.
— my shoulder.
— my arm.

7. My
— ears are ringing.
— fingers are tingling.
— toe hurts.
— vision is blurred.
— elbow hurts.

Narrative Completion

Fill in the missing word in each of the blank spaces of the narrative. Select the proper word or phrase from the words listed preceding each paragraph below. The same word may be used more than once.

go on living   valuable   inhale
humans   encircles   substance

1. Probably the most important _____ in nature is the air we
_____ . Air is a mixture which _____ the earth. To live,
all living creatures _____ this _____ air. _____
cannot _____ without air.

prevent   automated   maintain
keep   surroundings

2. Our _____ are important to us. We must _____ our air clean. Because we live in an _____ world, it is difficult to _____ clean air. In large cities we must _____ our _____ from becoming unhealthy.

way   is responsible for
be watchful   call

3. We _____ dirty and unsafe air "environmental pollution." The one thing that _____ most of the environmental pollution is the automobile. We must _____ of misusing this popular _____ of transportation.

disagree   topics   permit   relies
are contrary   condemn   beings

4. If people _____ their environment to become unsafe for life on earth, they will have no one but themselves to _____ for it. The air belongs to all living _____ in nature. Although people _____ with one another on many _____ , they must agree that life _____ on clean air.

clean   way   attempt
alert   depend

5. We must make a special _____ to keep our environment clean. We can _____ more on our legs as a _____ of transportation and _____ our friends against using the automobile too often. We can plant all kinds of trees and plants, which produce oxygen and help to keep the air _____ .

| stay | be passive | better | surroundings |
| part | expect | inquire | recognize |

6. When we _____ our _____ , we can always
    _____ about how we can _____ them. People cannot
    just _____ and _____ for their _____ to main-
    tain themselves. People must do their _____ to help keep it
    as clean as nature _____ it to _____ .

PICTOGRAPHS (WORDS IN CONTEXT)

Below are some drawings based on the dialogue presentation. Use the
word(s) or phrase(s) listed under each drawing to compose your own
dialogue. The same word may be used more than once. In addition to
the words given here, words of your own choosing may be used.

Active vocabulary: ache, tooth, ask about, complain about, count on,
ask for, patient, dentist, hear of, nurse, waiting, appointment

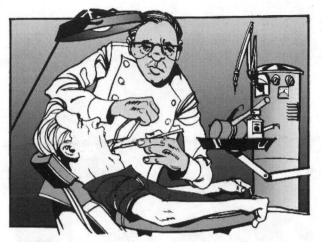

Active vocabulary: looks like, pain, feeling better, pills, mouth, relax, cavities, brush, account for, abstain from, result from, caution against, harmful food, sweets, drill, blame for, argue with

Below are some drawings based on the narrative presentation. Use the word(s) or phrase(s) listed below each drawing to construct a short narrative of your own. Words may be used repeatedly. In addition to the words listed here, words of your own choosing may be used.

Active vocabulary from paragraphs 1 and 2: element, environment, people, plants, animals, breathe, survive, maintain, precious, air, river, picnic

Active vocabulary from paragraphs 3 and 4: mechanized, guard against, unsafe, be responsible for, environmental pollution, automobile, beware of, means, allow, blame for, dirty, smoke

Active vocabulary from paragraphs 5 and 6: argue with, topic (issue), depend on, effort, rely on, caution against, pure, nature, ask about, improve, wish for, wait for, share, remain, clean, fountain, bicycle, couple

Crossword Puzzle

The puzzle below is based on the model narrative presentation. First, fill in the missing words in the sentences, then write them in the puzzle.

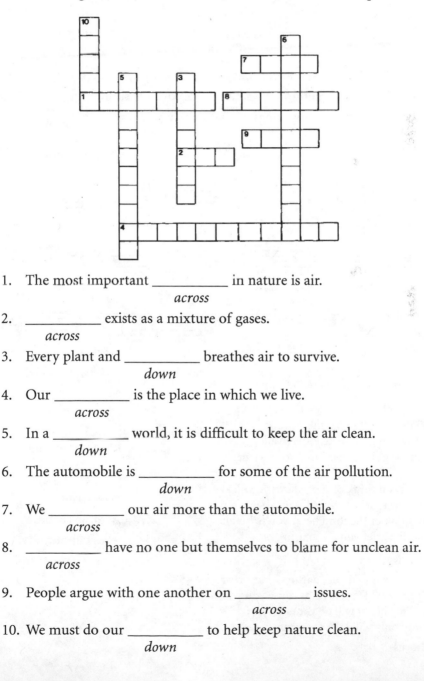

1. The most important _____ in nature is air.
   across

2. _____ exists as a mixture of gases.
   across

3. Every plant and _____ breathes air to survive.
   down

4. Our _____ is the place in which we live.
   across

5. In a _____ world, it is difficult to keep the air clean.
   down

6. The automobile is _____ for some of the air pollution.
   down

7. We _____ our air more than the automobile.
   across

8. _____ have no one but themselves to blame for unclean air.
   across

9. People argue with one another on _____ issues.
   across

10. We must do our _____ to help keep nature clean.
    down

Song

Below are the words and music of an old cowboy song. The cowboys lived and worked in the west between 1865 and 1890. Today, there are still cowboys who work on large cattle ranches. But their ways and work style are not the same as they used to be in the old days.

The North American cowboy was a carefree, happy person. He worked hard, played hard, and often had a special love for simple folk music. There are many cowboy songs available. Below is one of them.

Red River Valley

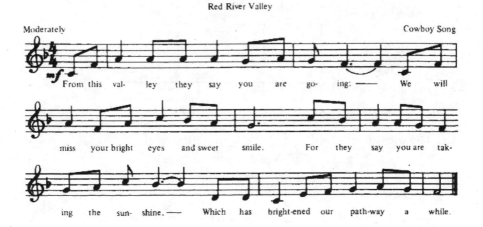

Moderately   Cowboy Song

From this val- ley they say you are go- ing: —— We will

miss your bright eyes and sweet smile. For they say you are tak-

ing the sun- shine. —— Which has bright-ened our path-way a while.

Chorus: (sung to the melody above)

Come and sit by my side if you love me,
Do not hasten to bid me adieu,
But remember the Red River Valley
And the girl that has loved you so true.

Won't you think of the valley you're leaving?
Oh how lonely, how sad it will be,
Oh think of the fond heart you're breaking,
And the grief you are causing me.

Chorus

I have promised you, darling, that never
Will a word from my lips cause you pain;
And my life, it will be yours forever
If you only will love me again.

Chorus

hasten: go quickly

adieu: goodbye

fond: loving

grief: worry

Answer the following questions:

1. Where is the cowboy going?

2. What will we miss?

3. What is the cowboy taking with him?

4. What should the cowboy remember?

5. How will it be in the valley?

6. How does the cowboy's girl feel?

7. What did she promise him?

8. What will happen if the cowboy loves his girl again?

GRAMMAR

Explanation and Examples

We continue here to study two-word verbs because of their importance and contribution to the living language. We must remember that two-word verbs are *verbs* plus *prepositions* in such close association that their new meaning cannot be inferred from the individual parts. Most of these two-word verbs should be learned in their proper associations. If we change these associations, we will change the meaning of the two-word verb unit.

The prepositional verb allows us on occasions to insert another part of speech between the verb and the preposition.

Examples: 1. **call on:** visit

Victor **called on** his friend before dinner.
Victor **called** early **on** his friend.

2. **call up:** summon
Steven was **called up** last week to serve his country.
They **called** Steven **up** to report at 7:00 A.M.

Generally, two-word (prepositional) verbs, such as **call on** or **look at,** differ from single-word verbs when each is used with its respective prepositional phrases. The two-word verbs allow pronominal questions with **who(m)** for personal noun phrases and **what** for nonpersonal noun phrases.

Examples: Victor **called on** his friend.—**Whom** did he call on?
Steven **looked at** the car.—**What** did he look at?

Also, many (but not all) two-word verbs allow the noun phrase to become the subject of a passive transformation of the sentence.

Examples: 1. The authorities **called on** the woman, (active)
The woman was **called on** by the authorities, (passive)

2. They **looked at** the car. (active)
The car was **looked at.** (passive)

Remember that frequently two-word verbs are highly idiomatic. Some of those idioms must be repeated in practice so that we can become accustomed to using them in proper context. Good examples of such idioms are such two-word verbs as **go over (homework),** which means to repeat or restudy, and **come by (the house),** which means to visit.

Below are more examples of two-word verb usage. The verbs used in Chapter 2 are presented here in the context of the model presentations. A more complete listing may be found in **Appendix I.**

abstain: **abstain from**—stay away from
You have to **abstain from** sweets.

account: **account for**—explain
How do you **account for** the many cavities?

argue: **argue with**—disagree with, be contrary with
I don't wish to **argue** that point **with** you, doctor.

ask: **ask about**—inquire
I **asked about** a good dentist.
ask for—request
I just **asked for** Dr. Greene's address, and here I am.

beware: **beware of**—be watchful
We must **beware of** misusing this popular means
of transportation.

blame: **blame (someone) for (something)**—hold responsible
for; condemn
You have only yourself to **blame for** it.

caution: **caution (someone) against**—warn
I want to **caution** you **against** some harmful food.

complain: **complain about**—express discontent with
I **complained about** it to my apartment manager.

contribute: **contribute** to—be responsible for
One thing that **contributes** the most **to** environmental
pollution is the automobile.

count: **count on**—depend on, rely on
My apartment manager told me I can **count on** Dr. Greene.

disagree: **disagree with**—be contrary with
I'm not trying to **disagree with** you.

fall: **fall in love with**—become enamored of
We can call this activity **"falling in love with** nature."

guard: **guard against**—be watchful, foresee and prevent
We must **guard against** making our environment
unhealthy to live in.

hear: **hear of (or about)**—know about (the existence of) someone or something
Have you **heard of** any other dentists?

look: **look at**–inspect
Let's **look at** the bad tooth.
look like-seem
It **looks like** we're having trouble.

refer: **refer to**—call
We **refer to** it as "environmental pollution."

refrain: **refrain from**—abstain from
You'll have to **refrain from** chewing anything that contains sugar.

rely: **rely on**—depend on, count on
We can **rely on** our legs more as a means of transportation.

result: **result from**—be a consequence of
Cavities **result from** eating too many sweets.

sympathize: **sympathize with**—feel for (someone), commiserate with
I **sympathize with** you, but you'll just have to do without it.

wait: **wait for**—expect
People cannot just **wait for** the environment to maintain itself.

Practice

Rewrite the sentences below. Use two-word verbs in place of the word(s) in bold. Read the sentences aloud.

1. I **inquired about** a good dentist.

   _____

2. I **requested** Dr. Greene's address.

   _____

3. Can I **delay** the treatment that long?

   _____

4. Well, young man, it **seems** we're having trouble.

   _____

5. Now then, let's **inspect** the bad tooth.

   _____

6. You'll have to **stay away from** sweets.

   _____

7. They are a **consequence of** eating too many sweets.

   _____

8. You'll have to **abstain from** chewing anything that contains sugar.

   _____

9. I **commiserate with** you, but you'll have to do without it.

   _____

10. I want to **warn** you, Mr. Garza, **against** some harmful food.

    _____

11. You'll have to **give something in return for** it.

    _____

12. I'm not trying to **be contrary with** you, doctor.

_____

13. The automobile is **responsible for** much of the pollution.

_____

14. We must **be watchful of** misusing the automobile.

_____

15. All life **depends on** clean air.

_____

16. We must **alert** our friends **against** using the automobile too often.

_____

17. We can call it **"becoming enamored with** nature."

_____

18. People must do more than just **want** the environment to maintain itself.

_____

Sentence practice with two-word verbs not previously introduced.
Fill in the blanks as indicated and read the sentences aloud.

Example: **cut in** (on)—join in suddenly, interrupt
     a. It is impolite to **cut in** on a couple dancing together.
     b. Joe **cut in on** the conversation.

1. **catch on** (to)—understand
     a. You've got to _____ _____ to driving a car before you can get a driver's license.
     b. It's not always I _____ _____ to my lesson.
     c. I can't _____ _____ easily to chemistry.

2. **check in**—return something, register
   a. Hotels want you to _____ _____ before 6:00 P.M.
   b. You must _____ _____ library books before they are overdue.

3. **cheer up**—make happy
   a. Your visit will _____ _____ your parents.
   b. Never forget to _____ _____ a friend.

4. **drop in**—to pay a surprise visit
   a. _____ _____ to see us whenever you're in town!
   b. My son _____ _____ often to chat.

5. **get in**—arrive
   a. When does your flight _____ _____ ?
   b. Ill be in touch when I _____ _____

6. **be through** (with)—finish
   a. I'll _____ _____ with my lesson by morning.
   b. Let's go to the movies when you _____ _____ with your studies.

7. **go on**—continue
   a. She can't _____ _____ this way any longer.
   b. Though life is hard, you must _____ _____ .

8. **look out**—be watchful, be careful
   a. _____ _____ when crossing streets!
   b. On the highway, you must _____ _____ for falling rocks.

9. **look forward to**—anticipate, expect with pleasure
   a. Students always _____ _____ the weekend.
   b. Professors _____ _____ summer vacations.

10. **run into**—meet by chance; collide with
    a. I usually _____ _____ people I haven't seen for a long time.
    b. If you're careless, you could _____ _____ a car.

11. **take off**—remove; leave
    a. The plane _____ _____ exactly at 2:00 P.M.
    b. When I want to feel comfortable, I _____ _____ my clothing.

IDEA RECOGNITION

Copy from the model narrative the sentences expressing the following:

1. Which is the most important element

   _____

2. How air exists

   _____

3. Who breathes air

   _____

4. Why we breathe

   _____

5. Where we live

   _____

6. What we must keep clean

   _____

7. Why it is difficult to keep the air clean

   _____

8. Where it is especially difficult to maintain a clean environment

_____

9. How we refer to dirty and unsafe air

_____

10. What contributes the most to pollution

_____

11. What people need to move from place to place

_____

12. What we must beware of

_____

13. What we need more than an automobile

_____

14. Whom people will blame for pollution

_____

15. To whom air belongs

_____

16. Who does the greatest harm to air

_____

17. What all of us must do

_____

18. What means of transportation we must rely on

_____

19. What we can caution our friends against

_____

20. What kind of love we express

_____

21. What we can plant

_____

22. What we can always ask

_____

23. How nature intended air to remain

_____

VOCABULAR Y ENRICHMENT

Paraphrasing

The following are **paraphrases** of expressions or words from the model narrative. Find those expressions, write them on the blank lines below, and repeat them aloud.

Example: I have an awful pain in my tooth.
            I have a terrible toothache.

1. a.   Air is necessary for all life.

    _____

    b.   No one can live without air.

    _____

2. a.   Our surroundings must be kept clean.

    _____

    b.   Large cities have a more difficult time keeping the air clean.

    _____

3. a. Cars contribute to unclean air.

   _____

   b. We can give up cars, but not clean air.

   _____

4. a. A clean environment is our responsibility.

   _____

   b. Lack of clean air makes it impossible to live.

   _____

5. a. We must try hard to maintain a clean environment.

   _____

   b. By growing plants and trees we show our love for nature.

   _____

6. a. Knowing about our environment is important.

   _____

   b. Everybody must participate in keeping our environment clean.

   _____

Lexical Units

Select the word(s) or phrases(s) from the words listed below that best complete(s) each of the sentences. One selection may be used more than once. Read the sentences aloud.

Example: Air is an important element.
           Everyone needs air to **breathe.**

allow	pure	unhealthy	guard
automobile	plant	keep	especially
depends	pollution	need	

1. People cannot survive without air. We _____ clean air.

2. Our environment is the place in which all of us live. We must _____ our environment clean.

3. In a mechanized world, it is difficult to keep the air clean. It is _____ difficult in large cities.

4. When we make air dirty, it is unsafe for breathing. We must _____ against making our environment _____ to live in.

5. People need a car to move from place to place. The automobile is a major cause of air _____ .

6. We need this means of transportation. But we need our air more than we need the _____ .

7. We have ourselves to blame for it, if we _____ our environment to become unsafe.

8. People argue on many issues. They must agree on one: all life _____ on clean air.

9. People need to become nature lovers. This means that we have to _____ trees and plants.

10. Trees and plants are necessary. They keep the air _____ .

Special Expressions

Below are some additional uses for the verbs introduced in the model presentations. They are used idiomatically. Practice the sentences, then compose one additional sentence for each new verb, using the verb in a context not previously expressed. Read the sentences aloud.

Examples: **account: on no account**—under no circumstances, definitely not
On no account are you to use this button. = sample sentence
On no account am **I** to move this table. = your sentence

on account of	— because of **On account of** his injury, he could not play.
on the alert	— watchful, cautious We must be **on the alert** for errors.
ask for it	— invite trouble, deserve the results I'm sorry about your poor grade, but you **asked for it.**
buy off	— bribe It is illegal to **buy off** the police.
care less	— not be at all concerned Susan could't **care less** about my troubles.
in care of	— in charge of; to the direction of Please mail your package **in care of** my office.
count (someone) in	— include (someone) If you're going out tonight, **count** me **in.**
count (someone) out	— exclude (someone) This game is too rough. **Count** me **out.**

die away — become fainter and fainter in the distance
We tried to listen, but the sound of his voice slowly **died away.**

die out — disappear; become unfashionable
Most clothing styles **die out** in time.

fall apart — be destroyed
The other day, his motorcycle almost **fell apart.**

fall for — fall in love with, become enamored of
Richard **falls for** every pretty face.

fall in — collapse, be destroyed; to form ranks
The earthquake caused the walls to **fall in.**

pay off — produce good results
If you study today, it'll **pay off** tomorrow.

pay out — make payment, disburse
The bank **pays out** a lot of money to its customers.

take off — leave rapidly; fly upward
The plane **took off** one hour ago.

work up — prepare a solution or answer; advance as a result of one's work

It'll take me a while to **work up** the ladder of my organization.

STEPS IN CREATIVE EXPRESSION

Write the two-word verb on the line. Read the sentence aloud.

Example: Josef worked up an appetite.   <u>*worked up*</u>

1. Bob asked about a good dentist.   _____

2. What are you complaining about?   _____

3. You can always count on Dr. Greene.   _____

4. They must have heard of you long ago.   _____

5. You must always ask for water in a restaurant.   _____

6. Are these people waiting for a bus?   _____

7. It looks like we'll have rain today.   _____

8. Don't look at me that way!   _____

9. I'm thin because I abstain from sweets.   _____

10. That's also how I account for good teeth.   _____

11. You must refrain from talking loudly in a library.   _____

12. We always sympathize with the poor and persecuted.   _____

13. I may disagree with you but still remain your friend.   _____

14. Please don't blame anyone for your own failures.   _____

Add new words and revise the sentence, if necessary, to suit the changes indicated in parentheses. Repeat the sentences aloud.

Example: **We breathe in** air. (He, inhale)
           He inhales air.

1. **People** cannot survive without **air.** (I, breathing)

   _____

2. **All of us** live in this environment. (She)

   _____

3. We must **keep** our environment clean. (maintain)

   _____

4. It is **hard** to maintain a **clean** environment. (difficult, pure)

   _____

5. We must **prevent** making our air **unhealthy.** (guard against, unsafe)

   _____

6. **The automobile** contributes to environmental pollution. (We)

   _____

7. **People** need air more than they need the car. (Everybody)

   _____

8. We must **beware of** misusing technology. (be watchful not to)

   _____

9. **All life depends on** clean air. (We all, rely on)

   _____

10. We must **count on** our legs more often. (use)

   _____

Review of Idioms

Fill in the blanks with the words given below. Read the sentences aloud.

working up	pays out	take off	fall apart
in care of	on the alert	fell for	buy off
on account of	died away		

1. _____ _____ _____his injury, he was absent.

2. A soldier is always _____ _____ _____ .

3. Mr. Harold tried to _____ _____ the official.

4. This letter was mailed _____ _____ _____ my uncle.

5. The echo slowly _____ _____ .

6. Rosi _____ _____ the handsome stranger.

7. Even when things go badly, try not to _____ _____ .

8. My _____ _____ time is almost here.

9. The employer _____ _____ the salaries of his employees.

10. I'm slowly _____ an appetite.

Create a dialogue similar to the model presentation based on the expressions below. (Lieu = L, Kim = K)

K: _____ have _____ toothache.

L: You should _____ dentist.

K: _____ recommend _____ good one?

L: I know Dr. Vincent _____ appointment.

K: _____ call for me?

L: Okay _____ find the telephone _____ .

K: Here's the _____ book.

L: I hope he _____ you right away.

K: I hope so too _____ worried.

L: We'll _____ someone else if _____ see you.

K: That's fine _____ the pain is _____ .

Vignette

Read carefully and learn the new words and facts. Discuss in class.

The North American Cowboy

1. Few people lived in the western part of America prior to the mid-
   nineteenth century. There were not many cities west of the
   Mississippi River. Growing crops was easy because the land was fertile. But there was no way the farmer could take his crops to the
   city market. The roads were bad, and the city was far away. That is

why the farmer had to think about raising cattle. When the cattle were grown and ready to be sold, they walked to the market.

2. The men who drove the cattle to the market were called cowboys. The ranchers hired cowboys to drive cattle to the market. The cowboys rode on horseback, keeping the cattle together all the way to the market. The cowboy was a hard-working man. He was strong and not afraid to ride through all kinds of weather. For his protection, he wore a handgun: the well-known "six-shooter." The cowboy did not remain in one place very long. Usually, after a last roundup, he would look for a new place of work. At times, the cowboy had to fight for his cattle: criminals tried to steal his cattle or wild animals attempted to kill small cows. The cowboy used his guns to save his cattle.

3. The cowboys gathered once a year to have a rodeo. The rodeo was a big show, a festivity. Cowboys always loved to sing songs about their work and their loneliness. Many people came to see the rodeo. Today, people tell stories and sing songs about the cowboys. Movies are made and books are written about the North American cowboy. Some of them are true, others are made up by the storytellers. Still, through these stories, the cowboy lives on as a romantic figure even as modern times have passed him by.

---

prior to: before
mid-nineteenth century: circa 1850
crops: food grown to sell
market: a place to buy and sell
raising: breeding; growing
drove: led, moved
rancher: farmer who raises cattle
hire: employ
protection: safety
roundup: collection of cattle into
    one place

steal: take illegally
attempted: tried
rodeo: a cowboy contest of skill
festivity: celebration
loneliness: sadness from being
    alone, desolation, solitariness
make up: invent
romantic: sentimental
pass by: go by, past

Discussion Questions

1. a. Did many people live in the western part of America before the 1850s?
   b. Were there many cities west of the Mississippi?
   c. Why was it difficult for the farmer to deliver his crops to the market?
   d. What did the farmer think about?
   e. When did the rancher take the cattle to the market?

2. a. Who drove the cattle to the market?
   b. What kind of man was the cowboy?
   c. How did the cowboy protect his cattle?

3. a. What did the cowboys do each year?
   b. What did the cowboys like to do?
   c. How do we learn about the cowboys?

4. a. Tell about some of the things the cowboy did on the ranch.

COMMENTARY ON MODEL PRESENTATION

Using key words and phrases from the model presentation, comment on the topics presented below.

element	mechanized	means
air	pollution	depend on
breathe	cities	caution against
mixture of gases	automobile	misuse
earth	transportation	nature
surround	guard against	be aware of
precious	beware of	wait for
environment		

1. a. Tell what people breathe.
   b. Discuss our environment.
   c. Express your views on the environment.
   d. Tell what you know about modern transportation.
   e. Write about why we must all help to keep the air clean.

2. a. Discuss the points in the model narrative that impressed you the most.
   b. Discuss the points in the model narrative that impressed you the most.
   c. Give an appropriate title to your composition.

FREE COMPOSITION

Directed Dialogue Improvisation

Compose your own dialogue based on the directed questions.

Example: Teacher: Romeo, ask Julietta if she's coming over tonight.
           Romeo: Julietta, are you coming over tonight?
           (Teacher = T, Student = S)

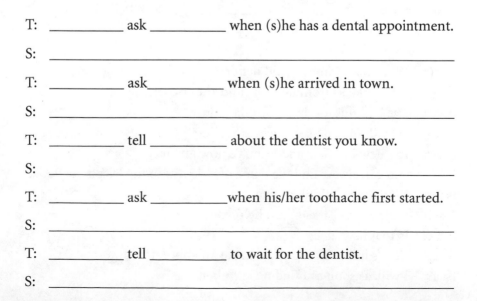

T: _____ ask _____ when (s)he has a dental appointment.

S: _____

T: _____ ask_____ when (s)he arrived in town.

S: _____

T: _____ tell _____ about the dentist you know.

S: _____

T: _____ ask _____when his/her toothache first started.

S: _____

T: _____ tell _____ to wait for the dentist.

S: _____

T: _____ tell _____ (s)he will have to wait.

S: _____

T: _____ ask_____ to come back tomorrow.

S: _____

T: _____ ask _____ if (s)he can come back another time.

S: _____

T: _____ tell _____ that you can come back another time.

S: _____

T: _____ tell _____ that you are sorry about the toothache.

S: _____

T: _____ tell _____ not to worry about it.

S: _____

T: _____ tell _____ goodbye until another time.

S: _____

Compose a short narrative, building on the dialogue below. Begin each sentence with _____ asks if, _____ answers that, or _____ says that.

Isaac: Where can I find a good dentist?
Jose: A few blocks from here, around the corner.
Isaac: I've had this toothache for days now.
Jose: Why didn't you see a dentist earlier?
Isaac: I'm new in town, and I don't know anyone.
Jose: You can always find the name of a dentist in the telephone book.
Isaac: Why didn't I think of that?
Jose: I hope Dr. Clarkson can help you.
Isaac: Is that his name?
Jose: That's him. But you must make an appointment.
Isaac: I will, as soon as I find his number.

Jose: I have to go now. I hope you'll feel better.

Isaac: I'll let you know how things turn out.

Jose: So long, Isaac.

Isaac: See you later, Jose.

Fill in the Missing Dialogue

For each of the drawings below, write your own dialogue which describes the action.

CHAPTER THREE

At the Drug Store

The Importance of Communication

IN THIS CHAPTER

Words to Remember
Compound prepositions introduced in Chapter 3

*according to — added to — ahead of — along with —
apart from — as for — at the time of — because of —
by means of — by virtue of — by way of — compared with —
due to — except for — for lack of — for the sake of —
from among — from behind — from between —
in accordance with — in addition to — in behalf of —
in between — in case of — in comparison to (with) —
in connection with — in contrast to — independently of —
in front of — in place of — in preference to — in regard to —
in search of — in spite of — instead of — in the course of —
on account of — on top of — out of — outside of —
regardless of — relating to — short of — together with —
with reference to — with respect to — with the intention of*

MODEL PRESENTATION

Dialogue: At the Drug Store

(Customer = C, Pharmacist = P)

C: I have a terrible cold. Apart from that, I have a headache. Can you suggest something I can take to relieve the pain?

P: Are you allergic to any type of medication?

C: I don't know exactly. I think that I can take most drugs except for strong pain relievers.

P: (Picks up a small box.) I recommend this brand for quick relief. In case of any complications, see your doctor.

C: Will this really help?

P: According to the label, you will feel better at the time of going to sleep. But if that doesn't help, then drink a cup of hot tea along with some honey. There's no miracle drug to cure a common cold.

C: Can you tell me where I can find some facial tissues? Because of all the sneezing, my nose is running terribly.

P: Over there, in between the cosmetics department and the first aid, is the tissue counter, right in front of row number 3.

---

apart from: besides, separate from
relieve: ease, reduce
allergic: have a bad reaction to
exactly: correctly, precisely
except for: with the exception of
brand: trademark
in case of: in the event of
complication: involved or confused condition
according to: as stated by

label: description of the drug
at the time of: during, while
along with: in addition to, together with
miracle: a supernatural thing or event
common: usual, everyday thing
because of: on account of
in between: in the area (time)
on account of: due to

C: Do you sell hot-water bottles here? On account of the fever, my feet feel cold as ice at bedtime.

P: We're out of them temporarily.

C: Do you have any cough syrup and lozenges?

P: You'd be better off adding some alcohol to your tea. In addition to making you feel better, it'll also make you sleepy.

C: For lack of something more suitable, I don't suppose you sell woolen socks to warm my feet?

P: Sorry about that. We don't carry that type of merchandise. You can get socks at a department store along with other things to wear.

C: I just know you're going to lose your patience, but I have to ask, how about some soothing cream? My nose hurts terribly.

P: You're in luck. Some new ointment just came in today. It's recommended in place of common cream, especially for an aching nose. (He hands the customer a small jar.) Try it, And, as for losing my patience, I can tell you in behalf of the management, the customer is always right.

C: That's very nice of you and the store management. I've driven for miles around in search of a nice place like this. I'm sure I'll be back, in spite of the great distance I have to drive.

---

out of: out of stock, unavailable

temporarily: briefly; for a limited time

be better off: (idiom) have an advantage

for lack of: in place of

suitable: appropriate

merchandise: things to sell and buy

patience: calmness, forbearance

ointment: fatty substance, salve

in place of: as a substitute or replacement for as

as for: referring to (something)

jar: container

in behalf of: speaking (acting) for someone else

customer: client, consumer

in search of: looking for

in spite of: notwithstanding; disregarding the difficulty or resistance

P: We're always happy to gain new customers, regardless of where they live.

C: You certainly made an impression on me with respect to merchandise and courtesy. I came with the intention of buying some cough medicine and just look at me now. I nearly bought up the whole store.

P: Never worry about that. There's more where this came from.

C: Thanks for everything. I'll be seeing you soon.

P: You're very welcome. I hope you'll get rid of the cold. Drop in any time.

---

regardless of: no matter what, irrespective of
with respect to: concerning, with regard to

courtesy: politeness
with the intention of: intending to
buy up: to buy all that is available
get rid of: discard, lose intentionally

Narrative: The Importance of Communication

1. Of all of the creatures in nature, the human possesses the most sophisticated means of communication. Communication may be placed ahead of many things we believe important in life. In fact, some people consider communicating as the highest priority for success. All human relations depend on effective communication: feelings, thoughts, anger, happiness, and sadness are all communicated by one person to another in their daily lives. For people, love is the most important feeling to communicate. If people don't communicate their love for one another, everything about their relationship falls apart.

---

sophisticated: refined
means: ability
ahead of: in front of, before
highest priority: of greatest importance

effective: active
fall apart: be destroyed
in contrast to: as opposed to, different from
gift: natural ability

2. In contrast to all other beings, people communicate most effectively when using their gift of vocalization. In addition to the use of their voice, people must make an effort to remain open to communication. Openness and honesty can work miracles in human relations. If people would remember to communicate honestly and matter of factly about their feelings, life would be much simpler than it generally is.

3. Oftentimes, misunderstanding does not only occur because of lack of communication. It happens when people want to hear something other than what they are told. Regardless of what someone says, people will interpret things relative to their own interests. This helps them to avoid doing something unpleasant or facing the truth. It is a kind of self-deceit practiced by many.

4. Much attention has been directed toward the many different gestures people make. It seems that while some gestures are used among many cultures, others are unique to one. For example, nodding one's head is commonly accepted to mean yes, and shaking of the head from side to side means no. Although these kinds of gestures signify yes and no in most countries, in India the opposite is true. There are many other gestures, called body language, which are interpreted differently by people of varied cultural backgrounds.

---

vocalization: speech, voice
in addition to: besides
matter of factly: truthfully
generally: usually
misunderstanding: disagreement, misinterpretation
regardless of: irrespective of, no matter
relative to: concerning, related to
avoid: keep away from

self-deceit: dishonesty with oneself
practice: repeat doing something
gestures: body movements
unique: peculiar, unusual, unequaled
nodding: moving the head up and down
varied: different
background: origin

5. We must distinguish between good and bad communication on every level of human relations. Wherever there is a problem, it surely relates to lack of proper communication. When this happens among friends, the persons concerned can correct the error and avoid trouble. However, misunderstandings or lack of truthful communication on the level of international diplomacy can cause many serious problems for the entire world. Let's always remember to express our opinions to others. No matter how contradictory our views are, in comparison to silence they are much more useful.

VOCABULARY

Dialogue Completion

Fill in the missing word in each of the blank spaces of the dialogue. Select the proper word from the words listed below. Read the sentences aloud. (Customer = C, Pharmacist = P)

along with	in spite of	be better off	out of
due to	in search of	merchandise	relief
brand	except for	in case of	because of
in front of	in between	apart from	in place of
relieve	allergic	regardless of	seeing

C: I have a cold. _____ _____ that, I have a headache. What do have to _____ the pain?

---

distinguish: show a difference, differentiate
level: condition, degree
relating to: applying to
proper: suitable, specific
concerned: involved

entire: whole
opinion: point of view, belief
in comparison to (with): compared with
useful: helpful, productive

P: Are you _____ ?

C: I think I can take most drugs _____ _____ strong pain relievers.

P: This _____ will give you quick _____ . _____ _____ _____ any complications, see your doctor.

C: Where can I find some facial tissues? _____ _____ all the sneezing, my nose is running.

P: Over there, _____ _____ the cosmetics and first aid, _____ _____ _____ row number 3.

C: I also want to buy a hot-water bottle. _____ _____ the fever, my feet feel cold as ice.

P: We're _____ _____ them temporarily.

C: Do you have any cough syrup?

P: You'd _____ _____ _____ drinking hot tea.

C: _____ _____ _____ something more suitable, I don't suppose you sell woolen socks?

P: Sorry about that. We don't carry that type of _____ . You can get socks in a department store _____ _____ other things.

C: How about some cream? My nose hurts from the constant sneezing.

P: You're in luck. We have a new ointment. It's recommended _____ _____ common cream.

C: That's great. I've driven many miles _____ _____

_____ a nice place like this. Ill be seeing you often, _____
_____ _____ the great distance from my home to this store.

P: _____ _____ where you live, we like your business.

C: Thanks for everything. I'll be _____ you soon.

Narrative Completion

Fill in each blank space in the text from the list of words and phrases preceding each paragraph. A selection may be used more than once, and more than one word may be used in one blank space. Read the sentences aloud.

effective	priority	ahead of	communication
communicating	relations	creatures	sophisticated
human			

1. Of all of the _____ in nature the _____ possesses the most _____ means of _____ . Communication may be placed _____ _____ many things we believe important in life. In fact, some people consider _____ as the highest _____ for success. All human _____ depend on _____ communication.

open	communicate	voice
vocalization	in addition	in contrast

2. _____ _____ to all other beings, people _____ most effectively when using their natural gift of _____ . _____ _____ to the use of their _____ , people must make an effort to remain _____ to communication.

self-deceit	relative to	hear
avoid	regardless of	misunderstanding

3. Oftentimes, _____ occurs not because of lack of communication. It happens when people want to _____ something other than what they are told. _____ _____ what someone says, people will interpret things _____ _____ their own interest. This helps them to _____ doing something unpleasant or facing the truth. It is a kind of _____ _____ practiced by many.

true   unique   gestures   commonly
opposite   attention   cultures   nodding

4. Much _____ has been directed toward the many different _____ people make. It seems that while some _____ are used among many _____ others are _____ to one. For example, _____ one's head is _____ accepted to mean yes, and shaking of the head from side to side means no. Although these kinds of _____ signify yes and no in most countries, in India the _____ is _____ .

problem(s)   persons   distinguish   truthful
error   relates to   level   nations

5. We must _____ between good and bad communication on every _____ of human relations. Whenever there is a _____ , it _____ _____ lack of proper communication. When this happens among friends, the _____ concerned can correct the _____ and avoid trouble. However, misunderstandings or lack of _____ communication on the level of international diplomacy can cause many serious _____ for entire _____ .

VOCABULAR Y SUBSTITUTION

Dialogue Completion

Fill in the missing word in each of the blank spaces of the dialogue. Select the proper word or phrase from the words listed below. Read the sentences aloud. (Patient = P, Doctor = D, Nurse = N)

instead of	drugs	bad reaction
unavailable	with the exception of	besides
in the event of	medication	in addition to

N: Next please! (Patient approaches.) The doctor will be with you in a moment. Come in.

P: Thank you.

N: Take a seat. Here comes the doctor now.

D: How are you feeling today, Kathy?

P: Well, doctor, I have frequent headaches. _____ _____ _____ that I have a cold. I've been sneezing all night.

D: Do you have a _____ to any type of _____?

P: _____ _____ _____ _____ strong pain relievers, I think that I can handle most _____.

D: I'll prescribe some cold medicine _____ _____ _____ _____ any complications, call my office immediately.

P: What if this medicine is _____ in my drug store?

D: That's not likely. But, just in case, let me give you a second
prescription _____ the first one.

P: Thanks a lot, doctor.

D: Take care now.

Narrative Completion

Fill in the missing word in each of the blank spaces of the narrative.
Select the proper word or phrase from the words listed preceding each
paragraph below. Read aloud.

| destroyed | in front of | greatest importance |
| active | ability | |

1. Communication may be placed _____ _____
   _____ many things in life. In fact, the human alone has the
   _____ to communicate like no other creature in nature. We
   give this communication the _____ _____ in our relations with people. All human relations depend on _____
   communication. If people don't communicate their emotions to one
   another, everything about their relationship can be _____ .

| usually | truthfully | ability |
| added to | compared to | try |

2. _____ _____ all other beings, people communicate
   most effectively when using their natural _____ .
   _____ _____ the use of their voice, people must
   _____ to remain open to communication. People who speak
   _____ about their feelings make life much simpler for others
   than it _____ is.

dishonesty with oneself   disagreement   keep away from
not paying attention   concerning

3. Oftentimes, _____ occurs not because of lack of communica-
    tion. It happens when people misrepresent things _____
    their own interest by _____ _____ _____ to
    what someone says. This helps them to _____ _____
    _____ doing something unpleasant or facing the truth. It is a
    kind of _____ _____ _____ practiced by many.

different   peculiar   body movements   distinct

4. Much attention has been directed toward the many different
    _____ _____ people make. It seems that while some
    _____ _____ are used among many cultures, others
    are _____ to one. There are many similar _____
    _____ which are interpreted differently by people of
    _____ cultural backgrounds.

compared with   involved   has a relation to
points of view   helpful   suitable
degree   differentiate

5. We must _____ between good and bad communication in
    every _____ of human relations. Wherever there is a prob-
    lem, it _____ _____ _____ _____ lack
    of _____ communication. When this happens among
    friends, the persons _____ can correct the error and avoid
    trouble. Let's remember to express our _____ _____
    _____ to others. _____ _____ silence, our views
    are much more _____ .

PICTOGRAPHS (WORDS IN CONTEXT)

Below are some drawings based on the dialogue presentation. Use the word(s) or phrase(s) listed under each drawing to compose your own dialogue. Words may be used more than once. In addition to those given here, words of your own choosing may be used.

Active vocabulary: cold, apart from, relieve, allergic, exactly, except for, in case of, complications, according to, label, feel better, at the time of, along with, cure

Active vocabulary: how are you, frequent headaches, besides, sneezing, bad reaction to, drugs, pain relievers, can handle, prescribe, prescription, not available, substituting, in the event of

Crossword Puzzle

The puzzle below is based on the model narrative presentation. First, fill
in the missing words in the sentences, then write them in the puzzle.

1. The human possesses the most sophisticated _____ of
   communication.   *across*

2. Communication is placed _____ of many things we believe
   important in life.   *down*

3. All human relations depend on _____ communication.
                                           across

4. People communicate most effectively when using their _____
   of vocalization.   *down*

5. In _____ the use of their voice, people must remain open
           across   to communication.

6. If people behave honestly, life would be much simpler than it
   _____ is.
      down

7. Regardless of what someone says, _____ will interpret things
   relative to their own interest. *across*

8. It is a kind of self-deceit _____ by many.
   down

9. People make many different _____ .
   across

10. Some gestures are used by many people; others are _____ to
    one group. *down*

Song

Below are the words and music of an old folk song. The name of the
song is "Down in the Valley." It comes from the Smokey Mountains
region. When a mountain man came to sing for his girl, he would recall
his lonely days in the valley to make his loved one feel sorry for him. Her
pity would soon turn to love, and the two would be happy ever after.

Roses love sunshine, violets love dew,
Angels in heaven know I love you.
Know I love you, dear, know I love you.
Angels in heaven know I love you.

If you don't love me, love whom you please,
Throw your arms 'round me, give my heart ease.
Give my heart ease, love, give my heart ease,
Throw your arms 'round me, give my heart ease.

Build me a castle, forty feet high,
So I can see him as he rides by.
As he rides by, love, as he rides by,
So I can see him as he rides by.

Writing this letter, containing three lines
Answer my question, will you be mine?
Will you be mine, dear, will you be mine?
Answer my question, will you be mine?

Write me a letter, send it by mail,
Send it in care of Birmingham jail.
Birmingham jail, love, Birmingham jail,
Send it in care of Birmingham jail.

Down in the valley, valley so low,
Hang your head over, hear the wind blow.
Hear the wind blow, love, hear the wind blow
Hang your head over, hear the wind blow.

Answer the following questions briefly.

1. a. How is the valley?
    b. What do we hear?

2. a. Who loves sunshine?
    b. Who knows I love you?

3. a. Whom should the person love?
    b. What does the singer ask?

4. a. How tall is the castle?
    b. What can she see from the castle?

5. a. How many lines are in the letter?
    b. What question does the writer ask?

6. a. To where is the letter addressed?

GRAMMAR

Explanation and Examples

Two or more words are often used as single prepositions. They are used as single units of speech. Such *compound prepositions* are particularly common in written English. Since they are mostly idiomatic, they must be learned in context. Compound prepositions (also called *phrasal prepositions* or *complex prepositions)* may be composed of various parts of speech. They may be two prepositions (i.e., **in between**), or preposition plus noun plus preposition (i.e., **for lack of**), or they may comprise an adverb plus preposition (i.e., **ahead of,** etc.).

Most of the complex prepositions belong to one of the categories listed below.

1. Adverb or preposition + preposition: **apart from, as for, out of, together with,** etc.

2. Verb/ adjective/ conjunction/ etc. + preposition: **because of, due to, outside of, regardless of, short of,** etc.

3. Preposition + noun + preposition: **by virtue of, for lack of, in accordance with, in place of, in spite of, with reference to, with respect to,** etc.

When you practice the sentences below, try to determine the parts of speech comprising each of the examples of compound prepositions. Here we offer only a few of the many useful compound prepositions in the context of their use in the model presentations. For a more complete listing of compound prepositions, see **Appendix II.**

according TO — as stated by, on the authority of
According to the label, you will feel better at the time of going to sleep.

ahead OF
— before, in front of
Communication may be placed **ahead of** many things we believe important in life.

along WITH
— in addition to, together with
You must drink a cup of hot tea **along with** some honey.

apart FROM
— besides, separate from
Apart from a terrible cold, I also have a headache.

as FOR
— referring to (something)
As for losing my patience, I can tell you, the customer is always right.

at the time OF
— during, while
You will feel better **at the time of** going to sleep.

because OF
— on account of
Because of all of the sneezing, my nose is running terribly.

except FOR
— with the exception of
I can take most drugs **except for** strong pain relievers.

for lack OF
— in place of
For lack of something more suitable, I want to buy some woolen socks.

in addition TO
— besides
In addition to the use of their voices, people must remain open to communication.

in behalf OF
— speaking (acting) for someone else
I can tell you **in behalf of** the management, the customer is always right.

in BETWEEN
— in the area (time) between
The tissue counter is **in between** the cosmetics department and the first aid.

in case OF — in the event of
In case of any complications, see your doctor.

in comparison TO — compared with
Even contradictory views are more useful **in comparison to** silence.

in contrast TO — as opposed to, different from
In contrast to all other beings, people communicate most effectively when vocalizing.

in front OF — located before, ahead of
The tissues are right **in front of** row number 3.

in place OF — as a substitute or replacement for
The ointment is recommended **in place of** common cream.

in search OF — looking for
I've driven for miles **in search of** a nice place like this.

on account OF — due to, because of
My feet feel cold as ice at bedtime **on account of** the fever.

out OF — unavailable, not in stock
Sorry about the water bottles. We're **out of** them temporarily.

regardless OF — no matter, irrespective
We're always happy to gain new customers, **regardless of** where they live.

with respect TO — concerning, with regard to
With respect to the merchandise, you certainly made a good impression.

with the intention OF — intending to
I came **with the intention of** buying some cough medicine, and just look at me now. I nearly bought up the whole store.

Practice

Identify what is happening by completing the sentences below.
Use words listed above your exercise. Read aloud.

in between	because of	relief	recommends
along with	terrible cold	allergic	cautions
facial	complications	thank	

You enter the pharmacy. You tell the pharmacist that you have a
_____ _____ . You ask for some _____ . The pharmacist asks you, "Are you _____ to any medication?" You reply
that you don't know. The pharmacist _____ a special brand of
drugs. He _____ you to call the doctor in case of _____ .
You ask about _____ tissues, _____ _____ the medicine _____ _____ your running nose. The pharmacist
points _____ _____ the cosmetics department and the first
aid. You _____ the pharmacist, and you leave.

Rewrite the sentences below. Use **compound prepositions** in place of
the words in **bold type.** If a compound preposition is in **bold type,**
substitute another in its place.

1. Communication may be placed **before** many things.

   _____

   _____

2. **As opposed to** all other beings, people communicate most effectively when using their gift of vocalization.

   _____

   _____

3. **Besides** the use of their voices, people must make an effort to
   remain open to communication.

   _____

   _____

4. **Irrespective of** what someone says, people will interpret things **concerning** their own interest.

   _____

   _____

5. Wherever there is a problem, it surely is **related to** lack of proper communication.

   _____

   _____

6. **Compared with** silence, opinions are more useful even when they are contradictory.

   _____

   _____

IDEA RECOGNITION

Copy from the model narrative the sentence expressing:

1. What the human possesses

   _____

2. Where communication may be placed

   _____

3. What some people consider to be communication

   _____

4. What human relations depend on

   _____

5. What is communicated by one person to another

   _____

6. How things fall apart in human relations

   _____

7. When people communicate most effectively

_____

8. What kind of effort people must make

_____

9. What can work miracles

_____

10. How people should remember to communicate

_____

11. When misunderstanding occurs

_____

12. Why people interpret things concerning their own interest

_____

13. What people want to avoid

VOCAL ENRICHMENT

Paraphrasing

The following are paraphrases of expressions or words from the model dialogue. Find these expressions and write them on the blank lines below. Read the sentences aloud.

Example: My head aches. = **I have a headache.**

1. I have a bad reaction to this drug.

_____

2. Can this reduce pain?

_____

3. I suggest this brand

_____

4. I am trying to locate

_____

5. Located before you

_____

6. They're not available

_____

7. It'll be to your advantage

_____

8. Wear something more appropriate

_____

9. I'll buy this instead of the ointment.

_____

10. I speak for the management

_____

11. I'm looking for socks

_____

12. No matter what happens

_____

12. The man was courteous

_____

13. I want to buy everything

_____

15. I hope you can lose it intentionally

_____

Lexical Units

Select the word or phrase from the words listed below that best completes each of the sentences. One selection may be used more than once. Read the sentences aloud.

Example: You must **communicate** with people.
           Communication is important.

communication	problem	self-deceit
silence	hear	matter of factly
other	relationship	people
open		

1. The human possesses sophisticated means of communication. _____ may be placed ahead of many things.

2. For people, love is the most important feeling to communicate. If _____ don't communicate their love for one another, everything about their _____ falls apart.

3. People use their voices to communicate. In addition, they must make an effort to remain _____ to communication.

4. Honesty can work miracles. If people would communicate _____ , life would be much simpler than it generally is.

5. Misunderstanding does not only occur because of lack of communication. It happens when people want to _____ something _____ than what they are told.

6. We often try to avoid facing the truth. It is a kind of _____ _____ practiced by many.

7. We must distinguish between good and bad communication. Whenever there is a _____ , it surely relates to lack of proper communication.

8. Our views are often contradictory. But in comparison to _____ they are much more useful.

Special Expressions

Below are some additional sentences using compound prepositions unlike those in the model presentations. All compound prepositions can be used in different contexts. Practice the sentences; then compose one additional sentence using the compound preposition in a context not previously expressed.

Example: **about-face** = turn in the opposite direction
Unable to convince the adversary, the leader of our team made an **about-face.**

about to   — ready to, prepared to
               When they knocked at our door, we were **about to** leave the house.

_____

all for   — completely in favor of or in agreement with
               Let's continue, I'm **all for** it.

_____

at first   — originally, in the beginning
               At first, all learning is hard.

_____

at last   — finally
               At last I am with my family again.

_____

bound for — going to
This bus is **bound for** New York.

---

bound to — likely to
Harry is ambitious; he's **bound to** succeed.

---

by ear — without reading music
Tom can play the instrument **by ear.**

---

by way of — via
We always go to Washington **by way of** Reston.

---

down and out — without money, destitute
There were times when I was **down and out.**

---

for ever and ever — always
Henry told his sweetheart he'd love her **for ever and ever.**

---

for keeps (real) — the real or actual thing; for always
This exam is **for keeps (real),** so pay attention and do well.

---

for the time being — temporarily, for now
My cousin will stay at our house **for the time being.**

---

from time to time — occasionally, not often, now and then **From time to time** it's good to relax.

---

in the face of — when confronted with
Keep your cool **in the face of** danger.

---

in time — within the required time, not late
We had a traffic jam but we arrived **in time.**

---

in tune with — in agreement or accord with
You are not **in tune with** progress.

---

in vain — without any result, futile
All his work was **in vain.**

---

of age — eighteen years or older
A person who becomes **of age** has the duty to vote.

---

out of date — obsolete, no longer in fashion
Her evening dress is **out of date.**

---

out of order — not working properly, broken
The soft-drink machine is **out of order** again!

---

up and about — able to move about (after an illness)
Sonia is **up and about** after her minor surgery.

---

up to date — modern, current
His clothes are always **up to date.**

---

upside down — inverted; disarranged; in confusion
The world of today seems **upside down.**

STEPS IN CREATIVE EXPRESSION

Write the compound prepositions on the line.

Example: I am about to study.   _____
                                                                        about to

1. Apart from that, I have a headache.   _____

2. I can take most drugs, except for
     strong pain relievers.   _____

3. According to the label, you will feel good.   _____

4. Take hot tea along with some honey.   _____

5. Because of the sneezing, my nose hurts.   _____

6. The counter is in front of you.   _____

7. On account of the fever, my feet are cold.   _____

8. We're out of them temporarily.   _____

9. Take this ointment in place of cream.   _____

10. I speak in behalf of the management.   _____

11. I'll be back in spite of the distance. _____

12. He drove for hours in search of the store. _____

13. Regardless of the distance, he found me. _____

14. He came with the intention of
    buying medicine. _____

Create a narrative similar to the model presentation based on the expressions below.

1. creatures / nature / human / sophisticated / means

2. ahead of / believe important / life

3. in contrast to / beings / effectively / gift of vocalization

4. in addition to / use voice / make an effort / remain open

5. regardless of / someone / interpret / relative / own interest

6. a kind of / self-deceit / practiced

7. some gestures / unique

8. problem / relates to / lack / proper communication

9. misunderstanding / lack of communication / serious problems

10. in comparison to / our views / more useful / silence

Vignette

Read carefully and learn the new words and places so that you will be able to answer all of the questions that follow this short presentation.

The Capital of the United States

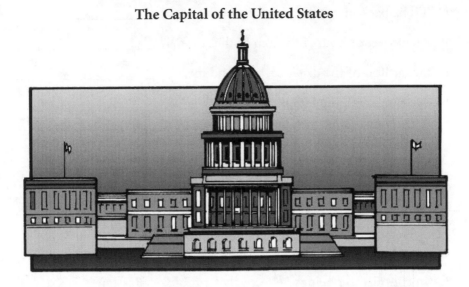

1. Washington, D.C. (District of Columbia) is the capital of the United States of America. To reach Capitol Hill, you must head on east along Constitution Avenue. At the foot of the hill stands the Grant Memorial. Capitol Hill itself takes in not only the 131 acres of the Capitol grounds but also the Senate office buildings, the three House office buildings, the Library of Congress, and the Supreme Court. The Capitol building has been the seat of government for more than two hundred years.

2. Washington is situated on the beautiful Potomac River. The city is known for its many monuments and museums. Of course, we have all heard about the White House, where the president and his family reside during the president's term of office. The White House grounds are situated not far from Capitol Hill, the well-known Washington Monument, and the Lincoln Memorial.

---

reach: arrive at
head on: continue
takes in: is comprised of

seat of government: place where government is carried on
reside: live
term of office: duration of a position

3. Complete the following expressions,

    a. Washington, D.C. is _____

    b. To reach Capitol Hill, _____

    c. At the foot of the hill stands _____

    d. Capitol Hill takes in _____

    e. The Capitol building has been _____

    f. Washington is situated _____

    g. The city is known for _____

    h. We have all heard about _____

    i. The president and his family _____

    j. The White House grounds are situated _____

COMMENTARY ON MODEL PRESENTATION

Using key words and phrases from the model presentation, comment on the topics presented below.

all creatures	success	person to another
nature	human relations	daily life
human	depend	love
sophisticated means	effective	most important feeling
communication	feelings	communicate
placed ahead	thoughts	everything
important	anger	relationship
people consider	happiness	falls apart
highest priority	sadness	

1. a. Discuss why communication is important.

    b. Tell what you know about the ways we communicate.

    c. Comment on what is most important in human relations.

    d.   List some nonverbal means of communication used by people.

    e.   Tell what can cause misunderstanding among people.

2. a.   Discuss the points in the model narrative that impressed you the most.

    b.   Discuss the points in the model narrative that impressed you the most.

    c.   Give an appropriate title to your composition.

FREE COMPOSITION

Dialogue Improvisation

Compose your own dialogue, using the situation given below and the new expressions you have learned.

1. You arrive at the drug store and you tell the pharmacist about your cold and headache.

2. The pharmacist suggests medication; he asks about switch to allergies.

3. You tell what you are allergic to.

4. The pharmacist tells you that the medication will make you feel better.

5. You ask about facial tissues and tell about your running nose.

6. The pharmacist tells you where to find things.

7. You ask about some ointment.

8. The pharmacist suggests cream.

9. You tell the pharmacist that you like his store and say good-bye.

10. The pharmacist hopes that your condition will get better.

Fill in the Missing Dialogue

For each of the drawings below, write your own dialogue which describes the action.

Compose a short narrative, building on the expressions below.

1. . . . the human possessess . . . may be placed ahead . . . human relations depend. . . .

2. . . . all other things ... the use of their voices . . . honesty can work miracles. . . .

3. often, misunderstanding does not only . . . what someone says . . . a kind of self-deceit. . . .

4. much attention has been directed . . . while some gestures are used . . . nodding one's head is. . . .

5. we must distinguish between good and bad . . . it surely relate . . . our views are. . . .

CHAPTER FOUR

A Friend Arrives at the Airport

Travel

MODEL PRESENTATION

Dialogue: A Friend Arrives at the Airport

(Joe = J, Mark = M)

J: Hi, Mark. What took you so long? I've been looking all over for you!

M: I've been waiting my turn to go through customs. How're you doing? How's Karen?

J: We're both okay. It's tough going through customs. How could I forget? How was your flight? Did you have fun in Mexico?

M: We ran into some rough weather, but on the whole it wasn't too bad. And the stay in Mexico was wonderful, only too short.

J: I'm sorry Karen didn't come with me. She sends her welcome to you. She suggested that you come over for dinner tomorrow.

M: That sounds good, Joe. What's up? Something special?

J: You're special, aren't you? It's been a long time since your last visit.

M: Say, Joe, I almost forgot. I have to call someone in a couple of minutes. I remember there was a phone nearby.

J: They used to have one near the ticket counter, but it's no longer there. Let's go look.

M: There's one over there. Okay, Joe, I'll see you tomorrow. Say hello to Karen. If there are any changes, give me a ring, okay?

---

all over: everywhere
waiting (my) turn: standing in line
customs: immigration procedures
flight: trip (by jet or airplane)
tough: very hard, difficult

on the whole: all things considered, generally
what's up: what is happening
a couple: a few
nearby: close to here
ticket counter: place where tickets are sold

J: I'm sure things will go okay. Do you think that you might not be able to make it?

M: I don't think so. But I'm a little tired now. It's been a long day.

J: I know, it's tough to travel-almost as tough as going through customs. But you'll be all right by tomorrow, won't you?

M: Sure, I believe so. I'm pretty tough myself.

J: Hey, I almost forgot. Are you bringing your girl along?

M: Oh, I imagine so. Wouldn't dream of coming without her.

J: We're both anxious to meet her.

M: We'll be there. Thanks for everything.

J: That's okay. So long, now.

M: See you tomorrow, Joe.

Narrative: Travel

give a ring: call up, telephone
make it: attend, be present at
bring along: include in one's
    company, accompany

anxious: eager
so long: farewell, good-bye

1. Only a short time ago, people traveled on horseback, by horse-drawn carriage, or walked on foot covering great distances. Travel from place to place took up much of people's time.

2. People have always dreamed of flying high up into space. Even as early as the Greek civilization, there were stories about how a person fash-

carriage: coach, vehicle
covering: traveling

distance: expanse, space between
    two points
take up time: consume time

ioned a pair of wings out of wax, fastened them to his arms, and tried to fly. He flew high up into the sky. But in his ecstasy, he flew too close to the sun, and the wax melted, hurling the unhappy flier through space as he fell to his death.

3. Failures did not discourage the inventors. They tried and tried again. The biggest obstacle, however, was the force of gravity which held, and still holds, man down on earth. But one day man really flew. What he had dreamed about for many centuries had now become a reality.

4. Just as the invention of the steam engine changed society, so did the coming of the jet age. The distances it took days to cover in the past are now traveled in a few hours. It took a ship two weeks to cross the Atlantic Ocean. Now, it takes only a few hours to travel the same distance in a jet. Who knows, someday it may take a few minutes.

6. Because of better travel conditions, all of the continents have also become closer to one another. In the past, people only heard or read about things in other parts of the world. Now they can buy a plane ticket and experience the enjoyment of seeing things for themselves.

8. But faster travel opportunities also made us realize that we must have more tolerance for one another. Our own globe is a huge ship

---

fashion: make, shape
fasten: attach
wax: substance used for making candles
ecstasy: feeling of great joy
melt: dissolve
hurl: throw or fling with force
failure: lack of success
inventor: one who creates things

obstacle: hindrance, difficulty
force of gravity: force drawing all bodies toward the center of the earth
reality: real, fact
invention: discovery, finding
steam: boiling water turned into vapor

hurling through infinite space; we are only travelers who share its limited area. We must learn to live together in harmony for the good of all people. And we know now that we must share all resources with each other, because their lack creates hardship for some people. And their hardship becomes our business too.

10. Finally, travel has given people the opportunity to test one another and to find out the truth about all people. We may be different in our customs, the color of our skin, or our religion. We may pursue a different life style. We may even differ in the way we enjoy music and art. In the end, however, we are all human. And being human means that none of us is perfect. How can any imperfect person say that she or he is better than another imperfect person? Let's travel some more!

VOCABULARY

Dialogue Completion

Fill in the missing word in each of the blank spaces of the dialogue. Select the proper word from the words listed below. One word may be used more than once. Repeat the sentences aloud for correct pronunciation.

dream	couple	travel	didn't	was
think	anxious	forgot	wasn't	been

---

cross: go from one side to the other, traverse
continent: part of the globe (earth)
opportunity: chance
tolerance: acceptance of differences in beliefs or customs
globe: earth
huge: very big
infinite: endless

limited: restricted, narrow
harmony: peace, agreement
resources: raw materials
lack: need, absence
hardship: difficulty
pursue: engage in, practice, go after
differ: be different, vary, not agree with
perfect: without defect

believe   might   ran   what's up   fun
won't   ring   sounds   took

JOE: Hi Mark. What _____ you so long?

MARK: I've _____ waiting my turn to go through customs.

JOE: How _____ your flight? Did you have _____ in Mexico?

MARK: We _____ into some rough weather, but on the whole it _____ too bad.

JOE: I'm sorry Karen _____ come with me. She sends her welcome to you. Can you come over for dinner tomorrow?

MARK: That _____ good, Joe. _____ _____ ? Something special?

JOE: You're special, aren't you? It's _____ a long time since your last visit.

MARK: Say, Joe, I almost _____ . I have to call someone in a _____ of minutes. Where's a phone?

JOE: Right there, at the ticket counter.

MARK: Thanks. I see it over there. I'll see you tomorrow. If you change your mind, give me a _____

JOE: I'm sure things will go okay. Do you think that you _____ not be able to make it?

MARK: I don't _____ so. But I'm a little tired now. It's _____ a long day.

JOE: I know, it's tough to _____ . But you'll be all right by tomorrow, _____ you?

MARK: Sure, I _____ so. I'm pretty tough myself.

JOE: Don't forget to bring your girl along. We're _____ to meet her.

MARK: I wouldn't _____ of coming without her. Thanks again.

JOE: That's okay. So long now.

MARK: See you tomorrow, Joe.

Narrative Completion

Fill in each blank space in the text from the list of words preceding each paragraph. A selection may be used more than once, and more than one word may be used in one blank space. Read the sentences aloud.

took	covering	travel
carriage	short	traveled

1. Only a _____ time ago, people _____ on horseback, by horse-drawn _____ , or walked on foot _____ great distances. _____ from place to place _____ up much of people's time.

melted	flew	fashioned	dreamed
flown	tried	were	have

2. People _____ always _____ of flying high up into space. Even as early as the Greek civilization, there _____ stories about how a person _____ a pair of wings out of wax and _____ to fly. He _____ high up into the sky. But in his ecstasy, he had _____ too close to the sun, and the wings _____ , hurling the unhappy flier to his death.

become	holds	was	tried
dreamed	held	obstacle	did
flew	gravity	inventors	

3. Failure _____ not discourage the _____ . They
_____ and _____ again. The biggest _____ ,
however, _____ the force of _____ which _____ ,
and still _____ , man down on earth. But one day man really
_____ . What he had _____ about for many centuries
had now _____ a reality.

| may | takes | took | changed |
| go | cross | are | invention |

4. Just as the _____ of the steam engine _____ society, so
didthe coming of the jet age. The distances it _____ days to
cover in the past _____ now traveled in a few hours. It
_____ a ship two weeks to _____ the Atlantic Ocean. Now
it _____ only a few hours to _____ the same distance in a
jet. Who knows, someday it _____ take a few minutes.

| seeing | buy | heard | come |
| experience | read | travel | have |

5. Because of better _____ conditions, all of the continents
_____ also _____ closer to one another. In the past,
people only _____ or _____ about things in other
parts of the world. Now they can _____ a plane ticket and
_____ the enjoyment of _____ things for themselves.

| share | have | realize | live |
| learn | harmony | made | |

6. But faster travel also _____ us _____ that we must
_____ more tolerance for one another. We are all travelers
who _____ the limited space on this globe. We _____
to _____ together in _____ for the good of all people.
We must _____ all resources with each other.

travel	human	may	test
say	find out	given	enjoy
perfect	customs	color	religion

7. Finally, travel has _____ people the opportunity to _____ one another and to _____ the truth about all people. We _____ be different in our _____ , the _____ of our skin, our _____ , our life style, or even the way we _____ music and art. In the end, however, we are all _____ . And being _____ means that none of us is _____ . How can any imperfect person _____ that she or he is better than another imperfect person? Let's _____ some more!

VOCABULAR Y SUBSTITUTION

Dialogue Completion

Fill in the missing word in each of the blank spaces of the dialogue. Select the proper word or phrase from the words listed below. Read aloud. (Greg = G, Vicki = V)

eager	close to here	trip
complete the plans	few	all things considered
call up	what's happening	immigration
standing in line	everywhere	departure

V: Excuse me, please, do I have to show my papers? I've been looking for the _____ official.

G: I've been _____ _____ _____ to go through _____ .

V: I've heard we have to show our tickets and our passports.

G: _____ _____ _____ , this isn't so bad. They're not searching through our bags. How was your _____ ?

V: Oh, it was okay. Look, over there! _____ _____ ?

G: They're checking some baggage. They won't do it to us. We only have a _____ suitcases each.

V: How about a cup of coffee? There's a restaurant _____ _____ _____ .

G: Sounds good. We've got another whole hour before our _____ . Say, when we get back home, can I _____ you _____ .

V: I don't see why not. Will you be able to _____ _____ _____ by the end of the month?

G: I believe so. I'm always _____ to travel, but I'm even more _____ to return home.

V: And now that I'll be expecting your call, I'll be _____ to return home, too.

Narrative Completion

Fill in the **proper form** of the missing **verb** in the blank spaces of the narrative. Select the verb from the verbs listed preceding each paragraph below. One verb may be used more than once. Read the sentences aloud.

consume   walk   cover   travel

1. Only a short time ago, people _____ on horseback or _____ on foot to _____ great distances. Travel from place to place _____ much of people's time.

fall   try   fly
melt   fashion   dream

2. People had always _____ of _____ high up into space. Many years ago, a person _____ a pair of wings out of wax and _____ to fly. He _____ high up into the sky. But in his ecstasy, he _____ too close to the sun, and the wings _____ . The unhappy flier _____ to his death.

become	fly	be	discourage
dream	hold	try	

3. Failure did not _____ the inventors. They _____ and _____ again. The biggest obstacle, however, _____ the force of gravity which _____ , and still _____ , people down on earth. But one day man really _____ . What he had _____ about for many centuries has now _____ a reality.

know	cross	cover	come
go	travel	take	change
last(s)			

4. The invention of the steam engine _____ society, as did the _____ of the jet age. The distances it had _____ days to _____ in the past are now _____ in a few hours. It had _____ a ship two weeks to _____ the Atlantic Ocean. Now it only a few hours to _____ the same distance by jet. Who _____ someday it may _____ a few minutes.

see	can	hear	experience
buy	read	come	

5. All of the continents had also _____ closer to one another because of better travel conditions. In the past, people had only _____ or _____ about things in other parts of the world. Now, they can _____ a plane ticket and _____ the enjoyment of _____ things for themselves.

create   know   inhabit   hurl

share   live   make   realize

learn

6. But faster travel had also _____ us _____ that we must have more tolerance for one another. Our own globe is a huge ship _____ through space; we are only travelers who _____ its limited area. We must _____ to _____ together in harmony for the good of all people. And we _____ that we must _____ all resources with each other, because their lack _____ hardship for some people.

Be(ing)   enjoy   find out   have

travel   differ   test   are

say   pursue   give   mean

think

7. Finally, travel has _____ people the opportunity to _____ one another and toone another and to _____ the truth about all people. We may _____ in our customs, the color of our skin, our religion, or our life style. We may even _____ in the way we _____ music and art. In the end, however, we _____ all human. And _____ human _____ that none of us _____ perfect. How can any imperfect person _____ that she or he _____ better than another imperfect person? Let's _____ some more!

PICTOGRAPHS (WORDS IN CONTEXT)

Below are some drawings based on the dialogue presentation. Use the word(s) or phrase(s) listed under each drawing to compose your own dialogue. One word may be used more than once. In addition to those given here, words of your own choosing may be used.

Active vocabulary: hello, been looking, all over, waiting, customs, flight, luggage, rough weather, on the whole, not too bad

Active vocabulary: what's up, come to dinner, sounds good, tomorrow, been a long time, couple of minutes, ticket counter, give a ring, make it, a little tired, tough to travel, wouldn't dream of, anxious to meet, thanks, so long

Below are some drawings based on the narrative presentation. Use the word(s) or phrase(s) listed below each drawing to construct a short narrative of your own. Words may be used repeatedly. In addition to those listed here, words of your own choosing may be used.

Active vocabulary from paragraphs 5, 6, and 7: continents, closer, better travel, parts of world, plane ticket, tolerance, space, together in harmony, share resources, opportunity to test, the truth, all are human, imperfect

Active vocabulary from paragraphs 1, 2, 3, and 4: travel, horseback, carriage, distances, people, time, dreamed, flying, wings, inventors, obstacles, gravity, earth, reality, steam engine, society, jet, ocean, train

Crossword Puzzle

The puzzle below is based on the model narrative presentation. First, fill in the missing words in the sentences, then write them in the puzzle.

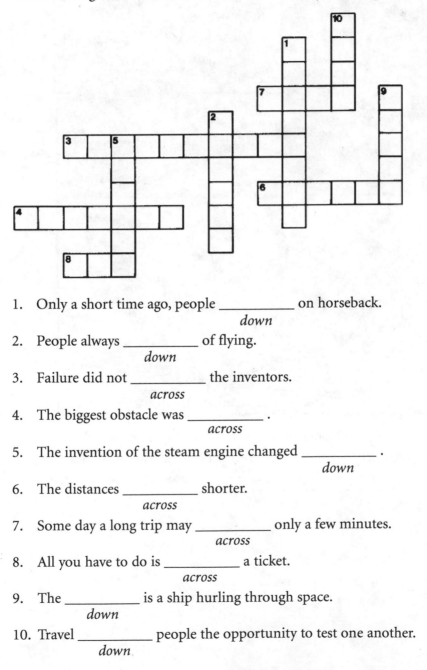

1. Only a short time ago, people _____ on horseback.
    down

2. People always _____ of flying.
    down

3. Failure did not _____ the inventors.
    across

4. The biggest obstacle was _____ .
    across

5. The invention of the steam engine changed _____ .
    down

6. The distances _____ shorter.
    across

7. Some day a long trip may _____ only a few minutes.
    across

8. All you have to do is _____ a ticket.
    across

9. The _____ is a ship hurling through space.
    down

10. Travel _____ people the opportunity to test one another.
    down

Song

Below are the words and music of an old folk song. This song tells us about a dying cowboy. It tells us that the dying man was once a happy, carefree person. He was shot during a fight in a barroom.

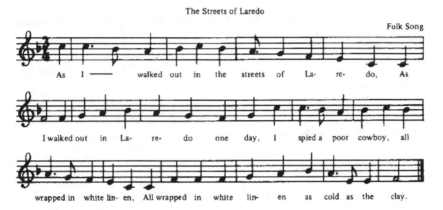

The Streets of Laredo

Folk Song

As I —— walked out in the streets of La- re- do, As
I walked out in La- re- do one day, I spied a poor cowboy, all
wrapped in white lin- en, All wrapped in white lin- en as cold as the clay.

Learn the words and sing together in the classroom.

2. "I see by your outfit that you are a cowboy,"
   These words he did say as I calmly went by.
   "Come sit down beside me and hear my sad story
   I'm shot in the breast and I know I must die."

3. "It was once in the saddle I used to go dashing,
   Once in the saddle I gallop'd away.
   First down to the barroom and then to the card
   house, Got shot in the breast, and I'm dying today."

4. "Get six of my buddies to carry my coffin,
   Six pretty maidens to sing a sad song.
   Take me to the valley and lay the sod o'er me.
   For I'm a young cowboy who knows he did wrong."

5. "Go fetch me a cup, a cup of cold water,
   To cool my parched lips," the cowboy then said.
   Before I returned, the spirit had left him,
   And gone to his Maker,
   the cowboy was dead.

6. (Repeat verse no. 1.)

---

outfit: suit, dress
calmly: peacefully
dashing: having a good time
buddies: friends

sod: turf, earth
fetch: get, bring
parched: dry

Discussion Questions

1. Who was all wrapped in white linen? Why?
2. How was the cowboy wounded?
3. What kind of a man was the cowboy once?
4. How does he want to be buried?
5. What was the cowboy's last wish?
6. What happened before the narrator returned?

GRAMMAR

Explanation and Examples

The base form of every verb is called the *infinitive*. This is the word we first look up in the dictionary: *be, draw, bring, hear, find,* etc. Additionally, most verbs have four other forms: the *present tense* form, the *past tense* form, the *present participle* form, and the *past participle* form. These forms we call the *principal parts* of a *verb*.

All verbs can show change in time by changing their letter structure. We call this *inflection*. Regular verbs have a standard inflection: walk—walked, talk-talked, dance—danced, etc. *Irregular verbs* have an **irregular** inflection. For example, we can show that there is a difference between the present and the past by spelling a verb differently each time:

Present	Past	Present	Past
becomes	became	holds	held
makes	made	finds	found, etc.

We call these verbs **irregular** because they do not follow a **regular** pattern of inflection. Some of the most frequently used verbs are irregular. Listed below are examples of the verbs used in Chapter 4. They are presented in the context of the model presentations. For a more complete listing of irregular verbs and their different classifications, see **Appendix III.**

	PAST	PAST PARTICIPLE	PRESENT PARTICIPLE

BE: **was**   **been**   **being**

I've **been** looking all over for you!

BECOME: **became**   **become**   **becoming**

What man had dreamed about had now **become** a reality.

BRING: **brought**   **brought**   **bringing**

Are you **bringing** your girl along?

BUY: **bought**   **bought**   **buying**

Now they can **buy** a plane ticket.

COME: **came**   **come**   **coming**

She suggested that you **come** over for dinner.

DO: **did**   **done**   **doing**

How're you **doing,** Joe?

DRAW: **drew**   **drawn**   **drawing**

People traveled by horse-**drawn** carriage.

FALL: **fell**   **fallen**   **falling**

The wings melted, and he **fell** to his death.

FIND: **found**   **found**   **finding**

Travel gave people the opportunity to **find** the truth.

FLY: **flew**   **flown**   **flying**

People have always dreamed of **flying.**

FORGET: **forgot**   **forgotten**   **forgetting**

Say, Joe, I almost **forgot.** Where is the phone booth?

GIVE: **gave**   **given**   **giving**
Travel **gave** us the pleasure of vacationing.

GO: **went**   **gone**   **going**
Now it takes only several hours to **go** the same distance in a jet.

HOLD: **held**   **held**   **holding**
The force of gravity **held** man down on earth.

KNOW: **knew**   **known**   **knowing**
Who **knows,** someday it may take a few minutes.

MAKE: **made**   **made**   **making**
Travel has **made** us realize that we must have tolerance.
He **made** a pair of wings out of wax.

MEAN: **meant**   **meant**   **meaning**
And being human **means** that none of us is perfect.

RUN: **ran**   **run**   **running**
I haven't **run** in days.

SEE: **saw**   seen   **seeing**
We can experience **seeing** things for ourselves.

TAKE: **took**   **taken**   **taking**
Travel from place to place **took** much time.

THINK: **thought**   **thought**   **thinking**
Do you **think** that you might not be able to make it?

Common Phrases (Uncommon Meaning)

Most common phrases do not appear in a dictionary. At best, one might find single words for each of them with definitions limited to their every-day usage. These phrases are presented here in the context of the model presentations. Occasionally, additional meaning may be expressed.

all over — everywhere; finished
I've been looking **all over** for you.
It's all over for us now. I love someone else.

believe so — think or imagine so
Do you have time for a cup of coffee?
Yes, I **believe so.**
Can you come to dinner tomorrow?
No, I don't **believe so.**

give a ring — telephone; call up
Give me **a ring** tomorrow about the meeting.
Joe **gave** us **a ring** yesterday.

imagine so — suppose or think so
Is Cindy a good secretary?
Yes, I **imagine so.**
Do you think there will be tickets left for the movie?
No, I don't **imagine so.**

make it — be present; accomplish or achieve a goal
We'll have an important meeting at noon tomorrow.
I guess, I'll **make it.**
I'm sorry, I won't be able to **make it.**

think so — believe or suppose so
Did you finish your homework?
Yes, I **think so.**
Is it going to rain tomorrow?
No, I don't **think so.**

Practice

Rewrite the sentences below. Change the **present tense** to the **simple past tense.** Read the sentences aloud.

1. People travel on horseback.

   _____

2. We run every day.

   _____

3. Evelyn is a very good astronaut.

   _____

4. Life becomes more difficult each day.

   _____

5. We buy groceries every Saturday.

   _____

6. Henry does his work with his friends.

   _____

7. The little girl falls on her face.

   _____

8. I fly to Dallas every month.

   _____

9. He forgets names easily.

   _____

10. Travel gives us much pleasure.

    _____

11. Families go on picnics.

    _____

12. He holds these things to be true.

_____

13. They know us well.

_____

14. Susan means to say that no one is perfect.

_____

15. Many people run for their health.

_____

Sample sentences using special expressions (**bold type**) are given below. Make up an additional sentence for each of the special expressions. Read the sentences aloud.

1. Sue looked **all over** for Mike.

_____

2. Do you want to go to the movies tonight? I don't **believe so.**

_____

3. I forgot to **give** Eleanor **a ring.**

_____

4. Is Pete a good soccer player? Yes, I **imagine so.**

_____

5. Do you have an important game tonight? No, I don't **think so.**

_____

6. Will you come to visit soon? No, I won't be able to **make it.**

_____

IDEA RECOGNITION

Copy from the model narrative the sentence expressing the following:

1. How people traveled a short time ago

_____

2. What took up much of people's time

_____

3. Who always dreamed of flying

_____

4. How the wings melted

_____

5. How inventors react to failure

_____

6. What holds man down on earth

_____

7. What had become reality

_____

8. How society changed

_____

9. What happened to the large distances with the invention of the jet

_____

10. Why the continents became closer to one another

_____

11. What happens when people travel

_____

12. What faster travel opportunities made us realize

_____

13. The size and nature of our globe

_____

14. What we are

_____

15. How we have to live with others

_____

16. What we must share with others

_____

17. How people can test one another

_____

18. What we all are despite our differences

_____

VOCABULARY ENRICHMENT

Following are paraphrases of expressions or words from the model narrative. Find those expressions and write them on the blank lines below. Repeat the sentences aloud.

Example: A short time ago people went from place to place. A short time ago people **traveled.**

1. a. Travel great expanses

    _____

    b. Travel was time consuming.

    _____

2. a. Flying high into space

   _____

   b. A person made a pair of wings

   _____

   c. He was thrown down to earth

   _____

3. a. Lack of success did not discourage .

   _____

   b. Gravity was a hindrance

   _____

   c. Flying became real

   _____

4. a. Something new changes society

   _____

   b. Travel quickly from shore to shore

   _____

5. a. The world is smaller

   _____

   b. With travel you live with the unknown

   _____

6. a. We learn to accept the differences

   _____

   b. The earth is a ship

   _____

c. Space is very big

_____

d. Peace is good for all people

_____

e. Raw materials are needed by all.

_____

f. Difficult times affect us all

_____

7. a. We have a chance to see others as they are .

_____

b. People have the right to go after their own customs

_____

c. No one is without defect

_____

Lexical Units

Select the word or phrase from the words listed below that best completes each of the sentences. One selection may be used more than once. Read the sentences aloud.

Example: Travel was slow in the old days.
          People traveled on **horseback.**

human	closer	fell
harmony	flying	wings
experience	force of gravity	travel
horse-drawn carriage		

1. It took people a long time to cover great distances. Only a short time ago people traveled by _____ _____ .

2. People dreamed of flying. One man fashioned _____ out of wax.

3. When he came close to the sun the wings melted. The man _____ to the ground.

4. People cannot fly. They are held on earth by the _____ _____ _____ .

5. People's dreams have become reality. The reality was _____ .

6. Society has changed because of the jet age. People have become _____ to one another.

7. People no longer need to read about distant places. It is now easier to _____ .

8. Travel makes people more tolerant. They learn about others from _____ .

9. The world has become smaller. People must learn to live together in _____ .

10. Because of travel, people meet. They find out that they are all _____ .

Special Expressions

Below are some additional irregular verbs unlike those used in the model presentations. They are used in different contexts. Practice the sentences, then compose an additional sentence for each new verb, using the verb in a context not previously expressed.

Example: **sell (on)**—convince of
           Mark **sold** me **on** the idea of reading. = sample sentence
           Gina tried to **sell** Julio on the idea of going to Florida. = your sentence

bite (one's) head off — answer in anger
You don't have to **bite my head off** just because I didn't come last night.

_____

_____

blow over — subside; become less serious
The situation will **blow over** soon.

_____

_____

break even — gain or lose nothing in a transaction
We sold the house for exactly what we paid for it. We **broke even** on the deal.

_____

_____

deal in — sell; do business in; be engaged in
Our college **deals in** learning resources.

_____

_____

draw interest — earn money on capital
Our savings account **draws** 7 percent **interest.**

_____

_____

drink up — finish a drink completely
Drink up, boys, we have to go!

_____

_____

eat out   — eat in a restaurant
                            Saturday night is our night to **eat out.**

_____

_____

get off   — leave any means of transportation
                            Joe just **got off** the plane from Santo Domingo.

_____

_____

sit out   — not participate
                            Thanks, I'll **sit** this dance **out.**

_____

_____

speak out   — express oneself courageously and freely
                            The senator **spoke out** for his people.

_____

_____

STEPS IN CREATIVE EXPRESSION

Write the irregular verb on the line. Read the sentences aloud.

Example: Gina came early this evening._____*came*_____

1. Don't bite my head off. _____

2. The situation will blow over soon. _____

3. The account draws big interest. _____

4. We like to eat out often. _____

5. You must speak out more frequently. _____

6. I hope we'll break even. _____

7. His business deals in bicycles. _____

8. We've sold our house. _____

9. The astronaut flew over Canada._____

10. It takes less time to travel. _____

Add new words and revise the sentence, if necessary, to suit the changes indicated in parentheses. Read the sentences aloud.

Example: **People** traveled on horseback. (Women)
              Women traveled on horseback.

1. Travel took much of **people's** time. (the business person's)

   _____

2. **People** always dreamed of flying. (Jimmy)

   _____

3. There **were stories** about Icarus flying on wings. (was a story)

   _____

4. Failures **did not** discourage the inventors. (never)

   _____

5. Gravity holds **man** down on earth. (us all)

   _____

6. **One day man** really flew. (Now, we are)

   _____

7. Inventions change **society.** (everyone)

   _____

8. It **took** fourteen **days** to cross the Atlantic. (takes, hours)

   _____

9. The **continents** have become closer to one another. (people)

_____

10. **You** can buy a plane ticket and **travel.** (we, go places)

_____

Substitute past time for present time. Read the sentences aloud.

1. Continents became closer to one another.

_____

2. People learned to tolerate each other.

_____

3. We heard about others.

_____

4. Mary bought a plane ticket.

_____

5. John flew a fast jet.

_____

6. We traveled to many places.

_____

7. They had tolerance for one another.

_____

8. People were equal in everything except knowledge.

_____

9. They learned to live together in harmony.

_____

10. Their hardship became our hardship.

_____

Create a dialogue similar to the model presentation based on the expressions below. Read the sentences aloud. (Peter = P, Felicia = F)

At the Airport

P: _____ been looking for _____ .

F: _____ been waiting _____ turn.

P: How _____ flight _____ ?

F: Not _____ occasionally _____ .

P: Karen _____ at home _____ .

F: _____ forward to _____ .

P: _____ coming _____ dinner

F: _____ urgent business _____ hope to _____ .

P: We'll see _____ tomorrow _____ .

F: Say _____ to Karen _____ for me.

P: Don't forget _____ at _____ for dinner.

F: I won't _____ .

P: See you _____ .

Vignette

Read the passage carefully and learn the new words and facts. Discuss the story in the classroom.

National Background of Americans

1. The first Americans who lived on the North American continent were the Indians. There were many Indian nations in North America. Now, there are approximately 300,000 American Indians left.

2. During the years following the discovery of America by Columbus, many people came to live in the New World. They came from many countries: England, Spain, France, Germany, Holland, Poland, and many other countries of Europe. They came to build a new life. They also came to seek freedom for their families. Some built cities, others farmed the land. As their population grew, the newcomers pushed the Indians from their land into reservations. This was the tragedy called "progress."

3. During the centuries following the American Revolution of 1776, many immigrants came to America. Wherever people could not stand the tyranny of their ruler, they emigrated to America. They came to the United States to be free.

4. Each nationality settled in a different area of the United States. The British mainly inhabit the East Coast. The French went west. The British called the East Coast New England. The french went as far as the Gulf of Mexico and called the territory Louisiana for their King Louis.

5. Germans, Scandinavians, and Poles settled in the North. Chicago used to be called the "Polish City." The Mexican immigrants settled in the Southwest, and the people from Africa lived mostly in the South. Many languages are spoken in our larger cities. But English became the official language of the United States of North America.

---

approximately: more or less
build: create, make
seek: look for
newcomers: recent arrivals
reservation: a place reserved or assigned
tragedy: misfortune
century: one hundred years

stand: bear
tyranny: cruel rule
ruler: monarch, leader
settle: establish residence
area: place, locality
inhabit: live in
coast: seashore
territory: land

6. People from Asia have settled mostly in the West. In San Francisco there is a section of the city called "Chinatown." In every walk of life, names are heard that betray the origin of the person: Mueller comes from Germany, DuPont from France, and Gonzalez comes from Mexico. Americans of different origins live side by side. The United States of North America is one country where people of different backgrounds, national origins, languages, etc., live and work together. Together they make America strong. Diversity of origin but unity of purpose makes a country strong.

---

used to be: was
official: authorized
walk of life: activity
betray: reveal, show

side by side: next to one another as neighbors
diversity: difference, variety
unity: togetherness
purpose: goal, aim, plan

Discussion Questions

1. a. Who were the first Americans?
   b. How many original Americans are there?

2. a. Who discovered America?
   b. Where did the people come from?
   c. What did the people want to build?

3. a. Who came to America after the Revolution?
   b. Why did the people come?

4. a. Where did each nationality settle?
   b. Where did the French settle? The British?
   c. What did the French name their territory? Why?

5. a. What was Chicago called?
   b. Which was the official language of the United States of North America?

6. a. Where did the people from Asia settle?
   b. What is a section of San Francisco called?
   c. What is heard in a name?
   d. What is the advantage to America of having all of those different people?

COMMENTARY ON MODEL PRESENTATIONS

Using key words and phrases from the model presentation, comment on the topics presented below.

carriage	dream	harmony
distance	steam engine	peace
covering	society	people
take up time	continents	together

inventor	closer	problems
obstacle	plane ticket	resources
travel	experience	hardship
gravity	faster	pursue
fly	opportunity	differ
try again	hurling	perfect
earth	tolerance	

1. a. Discuss how people used to travel not long ago.
    b. Tell how people travel now.
    c. Express your views about fast travel.
    d. Express your views about other people.
    e. Comment on how the world is becoming.

2. a. Discuss the points in the model narrative that impressed you the most.
    b. Discuss the points in the model narrative that impressed you the most.
    c. Give an appropriate title to your composition.

FREE COMPOSITION

Dialogue Improvisation

Compose your own dialogue, using the situation given below.

1. A friend has just arrived. He is late.
2. You are picking him up at the airport.
3. He had to go through customs.
4. You inquire about his trip.
5. He tells you that it was not too rough.
6. You invite your friend to dinner.
7. Your friend has some business in town.
8. You give him regards from your girlfriend.
9. He tells you that he will come and bring his girl.
10. You are both pleased and say good-bye.

Fill in the Missing Dialogue

For each of the drawings below, write your own dialogue which describes the action.

Compose a short narrative, building on the expressions given below.

1.   . . . a short time ago,. . . took up much time.

2.   . . . dreamed of flying. . . . Even as early . . . too close to the sun . . . through space, as he fell.. . . .

3.   failures did not discourage . . . tried and tried. . . .the biggest obstacle . . . force of gravity. . . . but one day . . . had now become a reality.

4.   . . . invention of the steam engine. . . . it took a ship . . . it takes only a few hours. . . .

5.   . . . all of the continents. . . people only heard . . . buy a plane ticket

6.   but faster travel... is a huge ship . . . learn to live together. . . we must share all resources. . . .

7.   . . . travel has given people ... being human means. . . . how can any imperfect person. . . .

CHAPTER FIVE

The Speeding Ticket
What Might Lie Ahead?

IN THIS CHAPTER

Words to Remember

Modal Auxiliaries

Meaning added to verb by modal auxiliary	*Present Time*	*Past Time*	*Future Time*
Ability **can:** *be able to*	*can write*	*could write*	*can write*
Necessity **must:** *have to*	*must write* *have to write*	*had to write*	*must write* *will write* *shall write*

**Obligation,
Advisability**

should: *ought to*	*should write*	*should have written*	*should write*
	ought to write	*ought to have written*	*ought to write*
shall:	*shall write*		

Permission

may: *can*	*may write*	*may write*	*may write*
might: *could*	*might write*	*could write*	*might write*
	can write		*can write*
	could write		*could write*

Possibility

may: *can*	*may write*	*may have written*	*will write*
might			*shall write*
will	*might write*	*might have written*	*may write*
shall			*might write*

MODEL PRESENTATION

Dialogue: The Speeding Ticket

(Wayne = W, Glenn = G)

W: Did you hear the latest?

G: You mean about the bank robbery?

W: No, about the traffic ticket Sue got yesterday.

G: Traffic ticket? How did it happen? Can't she drive well? Ha, ha, ha!

W: Don't ever say that to her! You might lose a friend forever!
And it's no laughing matter.

G: Well, I shouldn't really laugh. I got a ticket just the other day myself.

W: You should know better, Glenn. There are speed limits posted all over.

G: That's just it. I was too busy thinking about other things and didn't
see the signs.

W: If people would only concentrate on one thing at a time

G: Yes, I know. I keep telling myself how dumb it is for a grown man
to drive above the speed limit.

W: And the police will never tell you where there's a speed trap.

G: I don't think they should. Everyone would just slow down for them.
Then, they'd speed up again.

---

latest: news
robbery: holdup, theft
traffic ticket: summons for driving
　　too fast
matter: thing, subject
speed: velocity
posted: announced

busy: preoccupied
concentrate: pay attention
dumb: stupid
grown man: adult, grownup
speed trap: check point for
　　speeding drivers
they'd: they would

W: Can you keep a secret?

G: Try me.

W: I wouldn't admit it to Sue, but only ten days ago I paid a speeding fine at the exact location where she was caught.

G: Well, I'll be. As you can see, traffic tickets are quite commonplace.

W: But I really shouldn't get one. I know the traffic police wait for speeders at the corner of First and Madison Avenue. I should slow down.

G: Better luck next time.

W: It's not a matter of luck. It wouldn't happen if I'd pay more attention to the driving.

G: Go easy on Sue, eh?

W: I should be the last one to be angry, shouldn't I?

G: I know how you feel, Wayne. May I suggest something?

W: Go ahead.

G: Tonight, you should take Sue out to dinner and try to forget the whole thing.

W: I might just do that. Would you and Ellen like to join us?

G: We'd love to, but we can't tonight. Give us a raincheck, will you?

W: Okay. Maybe next week sometime?

G: Yes, we might try it then.

---

secret: something kept hidden to oneself

fine: penalty

I'll be: (expression of surprise)

commonplace: everyday thing

pay attention: be careful, look out for

go easy on: don't be angry with

suggest: hint

rain check: another chance

Narrative: What Might Lie Ahead?

Man does not live by bread alone. — Moses

1. Many ideas and thoughts have changed through time. People who lived one hundred years ago could not foresee many things of present everyday life that we take for granted. Traveling around the world in twenty-four hours, sending a man to the moon, and common motor travel were only dreams of yesterday.

2. There is one thing, however, that cannot change through the flow of time: the idea of education. The quest for knowledge has been present in every civilization since the beginning of time.

3. Education could be the key to solving some of the world's problems. There might be a possibility of establishing world peace if everyone in the world had an opportunity to become well educated. An educated world would be a place free from violence, corruption, and hatred.

4. Many people do not take the trouble to educate themselves. They blindly accept what others tell them without examining its wisdom. If they would only have confidence in themselves, they could achieve more in their lives.

---

changed: altered
foresee: know ahead of time, imagine
take for granted: accept as true
flow: progress
quest: desire
beginning: inception
solving: resolving

problem: difficulty
establish: settle, institute
free from: without
corruption: dishonesty
take the trouble: make an effort, try
blindly: without question
confidence: belief, trust
achieve: accomplish

5. As it is, people may often be misled and may even lose their basic freedoms. The Greek philosopher Socrates once said, "There is only one good, knowledge; and one evil, ignorance."

6. Finally, people should start believing in themselves. If they can't believe in themselves, no one else will believe in their worth. Self-esteem can only come with the knowledge of a person's accomplishments.

VOCABULARY

contribute = give **deeds** = actions **influence** = have an effect upon

A well-educated person may contribute to the growth of society. Even though a person might no longer be with us, his or her deeds would continue to influence the living.

VOCABULARY

Dialogue Completion

Fill in the missing word in each of the blank spaces of the dialogue. Select the proper word from the words listed below. One word may be used more than once. Repeat the sentences aloud for correct pronunciation.

can('t)	would(n't)	should(n't)
may	they'd	might
I'd	will	traffic
luck	dumb	robbery
I'll	signs	latest

---

misled: deceived
basic: fundamental
evil: wrong
ignorance: lack of knowledge

worth: value
self-esteem: self-respect
accomplishments: skills,
    achievements

WAYNE: Did you hear the _____ ?

GLENN: You mean about the bank _____ ?

WAYNE: No, about the _____ ticket Sue got yesterday.

GLENN: _____ she drive well?

WAYNE: Don't say that. You _____ lose a friend.

GLENN: I _____ really laugh. I got a speeding ticket myself.

WAYNE: You _____ know better; there are speed limits.

GLENN: I didn't see the _____ .

WAYNE: If people _____ only concentrate.

GLENN: I keep telling myself it's _____ to get a traffic ticket.

WAYNE: Of course, the police _____ never tell you about speed traps.

GLENN: I don't think they _____ . People _____ slow down and then they'd speed up again.

WAYNE: I _____ admit it to Sue, but I got the same kind of ticket that she did yesterday.

GLENN: Well, _____ be.

WAYNE: I really _____ get one. I know where the speed trap is.

GLENN: Better _____ next time.

WAYNE: It _____ have happened if _____ paid more attention.

GLENN: _____ Go easy on Sue.

WAYNE: I _____ be the last one to be angry, _____ I?

GLENN: I know how you feel. _____ I suggest something?

WAYNE: Go ahead.

GLENN: Tonight, you _____ take Sue out to dinner.

WAYNE: I _____ just do that. _____ you and Ellen join us?

GLENN: We _____ do it tonight.

WAYNE: Okay, maybe next week then?

GLENN: Yes, we _____ try it then.

Narrative Completion

Fill in each blank space in the text from the list of words and phrases preceding each paragraph. A selection may be used more than once, and more than one word may be used in one blank space. Read the sentences aloud.

thoughts	lived	present
for granted	foresee	could

1. Many ideas and _____ have changed through time. People who _____ one hundred years ago _____ not _____ many things of _____ day life. We take these things _____ _____ .

through	idea	quest
cannot	flow	thing

2. There is one _____ , however, that _____ change _____ the _____ of time: the _____ of education. The _____ for knowledge has been present in every civilization.

corruption	free from	could	might
would	educated	solving	establishing

3. Education _____ be the key to _____ some of the
    world's problems. There _____ be a possibility of
    _____ world peace if people had the opportunity to become
    well _____ . An _____ world _____ be a place
    _____ _____ violence, _____ , and hatred.

could   would   blindly   take the trouble

4. Many people do not _____ _____ _____ to edu-
    cate themselves. They _____ accept what others _____
    tell them. If they _____ only believe in themselves, they
    _____ achieve more in their lives.

ignorance   basic   misled
knowledge   may   can

5. As it is, people _____ often be _____ and _____
    even lose their _____ freedoms. Socrates once said, "There is
    only one good, _____ ; and one evil, _____ ."

infuence   accomplishments   can't
would   can   themselves
might   esteem   should
educated   worth

6. Finally, people _____ start believing in _____ . If they
    _____ believe in _____ , no one else will believe in
    their _____ . Self- _____ only comes with the knowl-
    edge of a person's _____ . A well- _____ person
    _____ contribute to the growth of society. Even though a
    person _____ no longer be with us, his deeds _____
    have an _____ on the living.

VOCABULARY SUBSTITUTION

Dialogue Completion

Fill in the missing word in each of the blank spaces of the dialogue. Select the proper word or phrase from the words listed below. Read the sentences aloud. (Pablo = P, Christina = C)

preoccupied	penalty	velocity
same	thing	be careful
stupid	an everyday thing	summons
something kept to yourself	check point	holdup
truly	news	

P: Did you hear the _____ ?

C: You mean about the bank _____ ?

P: No, about the traffic _____ Sue got for driving too fast.

C: How did it happen? Can't she drive well?

P: Don't say that to her! It's no laughing _____ .

C: Well, I shouldn't _____ laugh. I got a _____ myself the other day.

P: You should know better, Christina. There are _____ limits posted all over.

C: I was too _____ thinking about other things.

P: You've got to _____ when driving.

C: Yes, it was _____ of me.

P: The police don't tell you where there is a _____ .

C: Can you keep _____ ?

P: Okay. I can.

C: I paid a _____ at the _____ location.

P: Well, tickets are becoming _____ .

Narrative Completion

Fill in the missing word in each of the blank spaces of the narrative. Select the proper word or phrase from the words listed preceding each paragraph below.

accept   as true   imagine   altered

1. Many ideas and thoughts have _____ through time. People who lived one hundred years ago could not _____ many things of present, everyday life. We _____ many things _____ _____ .

inception   desire   progress

2. One thing, however, cannot change through the _____ of time: the idea of education. The _____ for knowledge has been present in every civilization since the _____ of time.

without   settling   difficulties   resolving

3. Education could be the key to _____ some of the world's _____ There might be a possibility of _____ world peace if everyone in the world had an opportunity to become well educated. An educated world would be a place _____ violence, corruption, and hatred.

accomplish   without question   make an effort

4. Many people do not _____ _____ _____ to educate themselves. _____ _____ , they accent what others tell them. They should believe that they can _____ more in their lives.

wrong   fundamental   deceived

5. People can be _____ often and may lose their _____ freedoms. Socrates said that knowledge is good and ignorance is _____ .

effect	give	respect
actions	achievements	value

6. Finally, people should start believing in themselves. Otherwise, no one else will believe in their _____ . Self- _____ can only come with the knowledge of a person's _____ . A well-educated person can _____ to the growth of society. Even after that person is gone, her or his _____ still have an _____ on the living.

PICTOGRAPHS (WORDS IN CONTEXT)

Below are some drawings based on the dialogue presentation. Use the words or phrases listed under each drawing to compose your own dialogue. Words may be used more than once. In addition to those given here, words of your own choosing may also be used.

Active vocabulary: hear, latest, robbery, traffic ticket, drive, friend, laughing matter, the other day, desk, window, phone, pencils

Active vocabulary: people would, concentrate, it is dumb, grown man, police, speed trap, slow down

Below are some drawings based on the narrative presentation. Use the words or phrases listed below each drawing to construct a short narrative of your own. Words may be used repeatedly. In addition to those listed here, words of your own choosing may also be used.

Active vocabulary from paragraph 1: ideas, changed, one hundred years, foresee, present, for granted, around the world, man on moon, motor travel, dreams, yesterday, can, might, bridge, skyline

Active vocabulary from paragraphs 2 and 3: education, common, no change, will, flow of time, civilization, key to solving problems, opportunity, free from violence, can, may, must

Active vocabulary from paragraph 4: take the trouble, may, educate themselves, blindly, others would tell, unable to examine, believe in themselves, achieve, might, have to, can, campaign, assemble, vote, elect

Active vocabulary from paragraphs 5 and 6: can, mislead, may, lose basic freedoms, Socrates, good, knowledge, evil, ignorance, start believing, can't believe, themselves, no one else, their worth, self-esteem, person's accomplishments, contribute, society, might, no longer, with us, deeds, would, influence

Crossword Puzzle

The puzzle below is based on the model narrative presentation. First, fill in the missing words in the sentences, then write them in the puzzle.

1. Many _____ have changed.

2. We take many things for _____ .

3. One thing that _____ not change is education.

4. Education _____ be the key to world peace.

5. People blindly accept what others _____ tell them.

6. They cannot examine its _____ .

7. People _____ even lose their basic freedoms.

8. People _____ start believing in themselves.

9. No one else _____ believe in their worth.

10. An educated person may contribute to _____ .

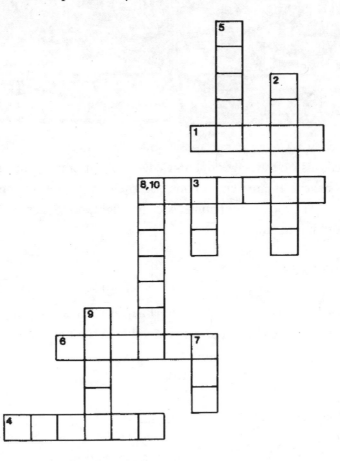

Song

Below are the words and music of a traditional cowboy song. In this song, the cowboy expresses his great love for the countryside–the vast space of the range where he spends most of his days attending the cattle. This is his home, and the cowboy "would not exchange it for all the cities so bright." Learn the new words contained in the song so that you can answer the questions following it. Sing the song aloud in the classroom with your fellow students.

Home on the Range

2. Oh, give me a land where the bright diamond sand
Flows leisurely down the stream;
Where the graceful white swan goes gliding along
Like a maid in a heavenly dream.
Chorus

3. How often at night when the heavens are bright
With the light of the glittering stars,
Have I stood here amazed and asked as I gazed
If their glory exceeds that of ours.
Chorus

4. Oh, I love these wild flowers in this dear land of ours,
The curlew I love to hear scream,
And I love the white rocks and the antelope flocks
That graze on the mountain tops green. **Chorus**

5. The red man was pressed from this part of the West.
He's likely no more to return
To the banks of the Red River where seldom if ever
Their flickering campfires burn.
Chorus

6. Where the air is so pure, the zephyrs so free,
The breezes so balmy and light,
That I would not exchange my home on the range
For all the cities so bright.
Chorus

7. Oh, I would not exchange my home on the range,
Where the deer and the antelope play;
Where seldom is heard a discouraging word
And the skies are not cloudy all day.
Chorus

---

bright: shining with light
graceful: having beauty, moving easily
leisurely: slowly
gliding: sliding
glittering: sparkling, shining
gazed: stared
glory: great honor
amazed: surprised, astonished
curlew: large wading bird
flocks: groups of animals
scream: yell
graze: eat grass
pressed from: driven from, exiled
flickering: burning unsteadily, as a candle in the wind
zephyr: soft wind
balmy: mild
discouraging: negative

Reply briefly:

1. Where does the cowboy want his home to be?

2. What is seldom heard there?

3. How are the skies all day?

4. What animals play there?

5. Where does the diamond sand flow?

6. How does the sand flow?

7. What does the cowboy love?

8. Who is the red man?

9. What will no longer burn on the banks of Red River?

10. Where is the air pure and the zephyrs free?

GRAMMAR

Explanation and Examples

Each **modal auxiliary** may express more than one meaning. A modal may be used by itself, i.e., "Can you do it, John?" "Yes, I can," or "I can speak English better than I can write it," *but* "A year ago I could write English but I couldn't speak it at all." A modal may also appear in the perfect form (Chapter 6), in a construction *modal + have + past participle*, i.e., "Tuet **could have done** it, but she didn't concentrate enough."

The *modal auxiliary* adds to the verb (which it modifies) a special, additional meaning, such as **ability, necessity, obligation, permission, possibility.** The modal has only two usable tenses, the present and the past: **can do, could do.** The progressive form is **can** or **could be doing.** The modal has a **perfect form (can** or **could have done)** and a **passive form (can** or **could be offered).** For the most part, the **present tense** is used for **future time: I might do it tomorrow.** Now we will discuss the various meanings which are added to the verb by the modal auxiliary.

1. Ability—can

There are three different kinds of **ability** expressed by the modal **can** (**be able to**). First, *can* expresses **physical ability** as in the sentence **I can breathe;** second, *can* expresses a **learned ability,** as when you know **how to do** something, i.e., **She can drive;** third, *can* expresses a more **general** kind **of ability,** implying that someone has the **power to do** something, i.e., **We can go out with you tonight.** This third kind of **ability** is used mostly for nonliving things, while the first two are used for living (human mostly) beings.

Examples: a. Wayne: Sue got a traffic ticket.
                Glenn: What's the matter, can't she drive well?
                Wayne: I can tell you this, Sue is a good driver.
                Glenn: Then why can't she watch where's she going?

b. What can I do today?

I can {
- relax all day.
- go for a ride.
- drive to Austin.
- read a book.
- invite a friend to my house.

c. Who can do it?
Mike — can lift heavy weights.
Sue — cannot lift as much as Mike.
Wayne — can lift heavier weights than Mike.

d. When can you come over to my place?

I {
- can come over on Tuesday.
- can't come over until next week.
- can come over after school.
- can't come over without mom's permission.
- can come over when I finish homework.

Note: In its negative form **can't** expresses **inferred certainty,** i.e., "Don't say that! You **can't** be serious!"

2. **Necessity — must**

There is only a small degree of difference between **necessity** and **obligation.** The modal **must (have to)** suggests an urgent course of action, like saying 'There's no other way, you **must** do your homework or else you'll fail the course."

We can often use the modal **should** (see below) to make recommendations.

Example: This car is in good condition. You **should (ought to)** buy it. But **must** is used in a stronger sense of urgency.

Example: This is an important chapter. You **must (have to)** study it. **Must** is often used to suggest that something is going to happen no matter what.

Examples: What **must (will) be, must (will) be.** **We must** obey the law.

Just the same, in its negative form, **must** will suggest that a certain course of action is **not** necessary.

Examples: You **mustn't** smoke. There's gasoline nearby. You **mustn't** spend more than you earn.

Must in its negative form often expresses prohibition.

Examples: We **mustn't** go through a stop sign. We **mustn't** play with fire. You **mustn't** do that!

3. Obligation, Advisability—should

The modal **should (ought to)** is used when we wish to make statements concerning our duty or an action which is to our advantage. However, we are given a choice to accept or reject the action.

Examples: **obligation**—what we are expected to do
We **should** wash our hands before eating.
or
We **shouldn't** stay out too late at night.

advisability—what is wise for us to do
We **should** slow down to 30 m.p.h. if we care about children.
or
We **shouldn't** eat so much if we want to be in good shape.

Oftentimes, **requests for advice** appear in the simple form of **shall,** as do expressions of **determination** and **volition. Shall,** however, is not a modal auxiliary but the equivalent of the verb **will,** indicative of future time.

Examples: Request for advice
Shall we go?   **Shall** we stay?
Shall we dance? **Shall** we?

Determination, Volition
We **shall** be back.   We **shall** overcome.
We **shall** help.   We **shall** continue on course.

4. Permission — may vs. can

In formal speech, only **may** is used to imply **permission.** However, in informal speech, **can** is often used for the same purpose. (Note: When the two modals are used in their past forms, **might** is more formal than **could.**)

Usually, permission is asked in the **first (I)** person or in the **third** (he, she, John, Mike, Mary) person.

Examples: First person—**May (can)** I use the bathroom?
No, you **may not (cannot)**.
Yes, you **may (can)**.

First person—**May (can)** I borrow your towel?
No, you **may not (cannot)**.
Yes, you **may (can)**.

Third Person—**May** (can) my friend come over tonight?
No, he **may not (cannot)**
Yes, she **may (can)**.

Third person—**May** Cornelia come to the opera with us?
No, she **may not (cannot)**.
Yes, she **may (can)**.

Permission with **may** can be expressed further with any pronoun form.

Examples: You **may** start now.
They **may** leave if they wish.
Joe's mother says that he **may** stay for the night.

Note: A simple request that does not involve permission can be constructed when using either **may** or **can:** May (can) I have a drink of water? This can also be done using the pronoun **you: Can (could)** you check out this book for me, please?

5.   **Possibility—may vs. can**

The English dictionary defines **possible** as something which "may or may not happen," or that "can be done, known, acquired, selected, used, etc."

May indicates a chance or the other possibility when used negatively: He **may** or **may not** arrive on time. **Can** suggests what is within the limits of possibility, frequently with a greater degree of **certainty.**

Examples: If there is a chance that things will go wrong, they **may (can)** go wrong.
I'm afraid something **may (could, might)** go wrong with his plans.

It is important to note that **could have** is used only for **past possibility,** not for ability in the past. **May** is not used in questions that express possibility.

Examples: Why is Hector late?
Could (might) he have missed his bus?
Can (could, might) he still be waiting for the bus?

Practice

Complete the sentences below. Use the correct modal auxiliary: **can, may, must, should, shall.** Then write one additional sentence using the modal from the example. Read all of the sentences aloud.

1.   Express **ability**

a.   Sue _____ drive well.

   _____

b.   I _____ stop on time.

   _____

c.   Some people _____ not concentrate.

   _____

d. When _____ you come to see me?

_____

e. _____ you go out with us tonight?

_____

f. No, I _____ . Sue is feeling bad.

_____

2. Express **necessity**

a. I _____ be at the office by 9:30 a.m.

_____

b. _____ you always interrupt me?

_____

c. We _____ all observe traffic laws.

_____

d. I _____ confess. Yesterday I got a ticket, too.

_____

e. You _____ laugh at Sue for getting a ticket.

_____

3. Express **advisability** or **obligation**

a. I _____ laugh at Sue, because I got a ticket too.

_____

b. You _____ know better, Glenn. There are traffic signs
all over.

_____

c. The police don't tell you where the speed traps are. I don't think they _____ .

_____

d. Traffic tickets are commonplace. But I really _____ have gotten one.

_____

e. You _____ always slow down.

_____

4. Express **permission**

a. _____ I borrow your car? No, you _____ not.

_____

b. _____ Rhonda spend the night? Yes, she _____ .

_____

c. Try to forget it. I _____ just do that.

_____

d. _____ I use the bathroom? Yes, you _____ .

_____

e. _____ Francis have a drink of water?

_____

5. Express **possibility**

a. I'm afraid something _____ go wrong.

_____

b. It _____ or _____ not snow tomorrow.

_____

c. Why is Hector late? _____ he still be at the station?

_____

d. He _____ missed the bus

_____

e. We _____ have to go and pick him up.

_____

IDEA RECOGNITION

Copy from the model narrative the sentences expressing the following:

1. What has changed through time

_____

2. What people could not foresee one hundred years ago

_____

3. The dreams of yesterday

_____

4   The thing that cannot change

_____

5. What has been present in every civilization

_____

6. What education would solve

_____

7. What possibility education might present

_____

8. How an educated world would be

_____

9. Why people accept blindly what others tell them

_____

10. What people must do to achieve more in life

_____

11. What can happen to people

_____

12. The thoughts of Socrates

_____

13. Why no one else will believe in people's worth

_____

14. How a person's esteem can come

_____

15. What an educated person can contribute

_____

16. How we remember great individuals

_____

VOCABULARY ENRICHMENT

Paraphrasing

The following are paraphrases of expressions or words from the model narrative. Find those expressions and write them on the blank lines below. Repeat the expressions aloud.

Example: Ideas and thoughts don't stay the same.
           Ideas and thoughts **have changed.**

1. a. During the last century

   _____

   b. In today's life

   _____

   c. Everyday car driving

   _____

2. a. One thing is unchangeable

   _____

   b. Getting educated

   _____

   c. The desire to know

   _____

   d. Present since the earliest days

   _____

3. a. Learning is a guide

   _____

   b. Possible to bring peace

   _____

   c. A world free from disturbances

   _____

4. a. People follow others without question

   _____

   b. If they would trust themselves

   _____

5. a. People can be deceived

    _____

    b. Their rights may be taken from them

    _____

    c. Lack of knowledge is wrong

    _____

6. a. People must have faith in what they do

    _____

    b. Confidence in oneself comes with individual achievement.

    _____

    c. A person's actions carry beyond his or her death

    _____

Lexical Units

Select the word or phrase from the words listed below that best completes each sentence. One selection may be used more than once. Read the sentences aloud.

Example: Many ideas have **changed through time.**
           Man **makes progress** as time goes on.

influence	victims
ignorance	violence and corruption
basic freedoms	peace
confidence	the idea of education
dream	for granted

1. A hundred years ago, people could not foresee the things we have today. Now we take these things _____ .

2. Today, we send a man to the moon. Yesterday, this was only a
   _____ .

3. One thing cannot change. That thing is _____ .

4. Education is the key to some of our problems. It might make
   _____ possible.

5. If all people would seek education, they might forget about
   _____ .

6. Some people do not educate themselves. They become _____
   of others.

7. Without education, people have no _____ in themselves.

8. It is not good to remain ignorant. It may lead to the loss of
   _____ .

9. There is only one good, knowledge; and one evil, _____ .

10. A well-educated person can contribute to the growth of society. Even
    after one's death, his thoughts and deeds _____ the living.

Special Expressions

Below are some additional expressions using modal auxiliaries. They
are used in different contexts. Practice the sentences, then compose one
additional sentence for each modal offered here, using it in a context
not expressed previously.

Example: **can't put one's finger on** =
can't locate immediately; can't find the answer

I know I've got that book, but **I can't put my finger on** it
right now. = sample sentence

He's learned that thing many times, but he **can't put his
finger on** the right answer. = your sentence

1. Ability

   a. If you can't drive, don't practice on the highway.

   _____

   b. You can do it, if you'd only try harder.

   _____

   c. We can't afford these high prices.

   _____

   d. You think I can't spell? I'll show you that I can.

   _____

   e. I like this school. I can be happy here.

   _____

2. Necessity

   a. Must I come inside? You'd better, if you want to eat.

   _____

   b. You mustn't think badly of Margo.

   _____

   c. I must go now, else I'll be late.

   _____

   d. We must do this again! It was great fun!

   _____

   e. We must take care of our chores.

   _____

3. Obligation/Advisability

    a. You should wash your hands before eating.

    _____

    b. Children should be careful crossing streets.

    _____

    c. People should care about people.

    _____

    d. I should write more often to my friends.

    _____

    e. Nora should start a diet.

    _____

4. Permission

    a. May I enter? Yes, you may.

    _____

    b. May I ask you a question?

    _____

    c. May I talk with Henry for a few minutes?

    _____

    d. May I have this dance?

    _____

    e. I lost Fidelio's hat. May I look for it?

    _____

5. Possibility

   a.   It may or may not rain tonight.

   _____

   b.   You're driving too fast. You may get a ticket.

   _____

   c.   He may be in late tonight.

   _____

   d.   We may have to do without bread for a while.

   _____

   e.   Weldon may have to catch a later flight.

   _____

Guess the Idea

Below are some clues about situations. Let's guess what happens during or after these happenings. Things may seem completely certain, but still we're not altogether sure they really happened that way. Do you get the idea?

Example: We are in New York City. We see on the street a man wearing a cowboy outfit. Guess: He might be a cowboy, (possibility) He can't be a New Yorker, (possibility)

1.   My friend Irma stayed up all night.

   _____

2.   Harry has just completed a ten kilometer run.

   _____

3.   Wayne's wife just got a traffic ticket.

   _____

4. Glenn is laughing about Sue's ticket.

_____

5. Sue did not pay attention to the speed limit.

_____

6. The sun is shining now, but the sidewalk is wet.

_____

7. The police caught Glenn speeding.

_____

8. Sue appeared in court yesterday.

_____

9. Wayne is angry with Sue.

_____

10. Ellen and Glenn ask for a rain check to go out with Sue and Wayne.

_____

STEPS IN CREATIVE EXPRESSION

Write the modal auxiliary on the line. Read the sentence aloud.

Example: Carlos is late. Shouldn't we wait?   _____*shouldn't*_____

1. I can drive a truck.   _____

2. Helen might come today.   _____

3. Pablo should write home often.   _____

4. Imatsuji might not know his way.   _____

5. I can do it as well as you.   _____

6. May I go to the movies?   _____

7. We should stop at a red traffic light.   _____

8. There must be a way to do this.   _____

9. Shall we order?   _____

10. Everyone can work.   _____

Add new words and revise the sentence, if necessary, to suit the changes indicated in parentheses. Read the sentences aloud.

Example: **Many ideas** and **thoughts** have changed. (People, countries)
             People and countries have changed.

1. **They** could not foresee many **things.** (We, changes)

    _____

2. **We** take many things for granted. (I)

    _____

3. **Susan** travels to many places. (Sue and Jerry)

    _____

4. **Motor travel** was the dream of yesterday. (Many things)

    _____

5. **The idea** of education cannot change. (Noble ideas)

    _____

6. **Education** is the key to **peace.** (Learning, progress)

    _____

7. **Individuals** should want to be educated. (All people)

    _____

Insert the modal of the category given in **bold type.** Repeat the sentences aloud.

Example: If you ____**can't**____ drive, don't practice on the street.
                  ability

1. Don't give him the car keys. I don't think he _____ drive.
                                                    ability

2. You _____ think badly of your friends.
         necessity

3. Henry thinks I _____ spell. I'll show him I _____ .
                  ability   **ability**

4. You _____ wash your hands before eating.
         advisability

5. I _____ write more often to my parents.
      advisability

6. Children _____ be careful crossing streets.
           advisability

7. _____ I enter? Yes, you _____ .
     permission   **permission**

8. I _____ go now, else I'll be late.
       necessity

9. You _____ do it as well as anyone.
         ability

10. I like this town. I think I _____ be happy here.
                         ability

11. People _____ care for the needy.
         advisability

12. We _____ have to do without oil in the future.
        possibility

13. Weldon _____ have to catch a later flight.
         possibility

14. David _____ be in late tonight.
        possibility

15. _____ I speak to you for one moment?
     permission

Create a dialogue similar to the model presentation based on the expressions below. (Imatsuji = I, Hiromi = H)

I: _____ hear the latest?

H: You mean _____ .

I: No, that's not _____ .

H: _____ how did it _____ .

I: _____ shouldn't really laugh _____ .

H: _____ should know better _____ .

I: _____ busy thinking _____ other things _____ .

H: _____ would only watch _____ .

I: _____ keep telling _____ .

H: Sorry _____ more careful _____ .

I: _____ the police _____ speed trap _____ .

H: _____ quite commonplace _____

I: But _____ shouldn't have gotten _____ .

H: _____ luck next time _____ .

I: _____ matter of luck _____ happened _____ paid attention _____ .

H: Anyhow _____ take Sue out _____ .

I: I will. _____ you come along?

H: No. _____ busy _____ maybe another time.

I: Sorry. _____ be seeing you.

H: So long. _____ see _____ later.

COMMENTARY ON MODEL PRESENTATION

Using key words and phrases from the model narrative, comment about the topics presented below.

ideas and thoughts	civilization	knowledge
through time	beginning of time	ignorance
foresee	establish world peace	belief in oneself
everyday life	opportunity	self-esteem
traveling around	free from violence	knowledge of a person's
the world	take trouble	accomplishments
man on the moon	confidence	deeds
influence	dreams	basic freedoms
the living	idea of education	

1. a. Tell about the changes.
   b. Discuss what does not change.
   c. Express your views about the need of education for all.
   d. Express your views about the basic freedoms.
   e. Tell how we can achieve peace.

2. a. Discuss the points in the model narrative that impressed you the most.
   b. Discuss the points in the model narrative that impressed you the most.
   c. Give an appropriate title to your composition.

FREE COMPOSITION

Dialogue Improvisation

Compose your own dialogue, using the situation given below.

1. You meet a friend on the street
2. You invite your friend to a cafe
3. Your friend heard about your traffic ticket
4. You don't want to tell him/her about it
5. Your friend laughs at you
6. You tell your friend not to laugh because it could happen to him/her.
7. You ask your friend to take you to the courthouse tomorrow
8. Your friend offers to take you
9. You make a definite date
10. You say your good-byes

Fill in the Missing Dialogue

For each of the drawings below, write your own dialogue which describes the action.

Compose a short narrative, building on the expressions given below.

1. . . . and thoughts have changed . . . who lived one hundred years ago . . . around the world . . . a man to the moon. . . .

2. . . . one thing, however, . . . cannot change. . . . the quest . . . been present . . . beginning of time.

3. . . . could be the key . . . world's problems. . . be a possibility . . . world peace. . . . an educated . . . free from corruption. . . .

4. many people . . . trouble to. . . . they blindly accepted . . . examining . . . have confidence . . . achieve more. . . .

5. . . . be misled often . . . lose their basic . . . is only one good . . . one evil. . . .

6. . . . should start . . . can't believe . . . in their worth . . . self-esteem can . . . the knowledge . . . accomplishments. . . . educated person . . . growth of society . . . even though . . . with us... deeds would . . . influence. . . .

CHAPTER SIX

Tell It to the Judge
He Should Have Listened

Words to Remember

advisability — *volition* — *conditional* —
conditioned result — *habitual customary action* —
inferred certainty — *inferred probability* — *possibility*
— *permission* — *request* — *prediction* — *ability*

Modal perfects

should   **might**   *would*   **could**

might *have*
should *have*   **advisability, volition**
could *have*

could *have*   **conditioned result**
would *have*   **(hypothetical statement)**

must *have*	**inferred certainty**
can't have	
should *have*	**inferred probability**
may *have*	
could have	**possibility, permission**
can have	**request**
can *have*	
will have	**prediction, ability**
shall, have	

The construction of the modal perfect:
Modal + have + Past Participle

MODEL PRESENTATION

Dialogue: Tell It to the Judge
(Judge = J, Sue = S)

J: All motorists know that they must obey the speed limits. You must have been daydreaming when you exceeded yours.

S: But, your honor, I . . .

J: You should not interrupt while I speak, young lady. I will tell you when to speak.

S: Yes, your honor.

J: As I said, you should have paid more attention to the road and the traffic signs. Had you done that, you would not have gotten the speeding ticket. Now, what do you have to say for yourself?

S: I know I should have been more careful, your honor. I could have caused an accident and hurt people.

J: The court will consider your admission of guilt.

S: I'll be more careful in the future. I'm sorry, your honor.

J: I wouldn't be in a hurry when driving, if I were you, young lady. At least you might have slowed down in a school zone.

S: Oh, but I wasn't in a hurry, your honor.

---

motorist: driver
obey: follow commands
speed: velocity
daydream: have pleasant thoughts
exceed: go beyond
interrupt: to break in on
   someone's talk
pay attention to: listen to

traffic sign: road signal
accident: unfortunate event
   resulting from carelessness;
   mishap
consider: keep in mind
admission: confession
guilt: fault, error
zone: section, area

J: Then why would you be getting this speeding fine? You must have been speeding. That's what the police report says, and also the witness.

S: It isn't because of speeding, your honor, but because I wasn't careful enough.

J: And what would you mean by that?

S: Well, you see, your honor, it's like this. Many of my friends drive faster than the speed limit most of the time, only they never get caught at it.

J: How's that?

S: They've been driving long enough to know where the speed traps are.

J: What? Would you repeat that?

S: They do, your honor. And they've warned me about the one that caught me. I should have listened.

J: Enough! You've gone too far, young woman. That'll be fifty-five dollars fine plus damages to the other car and truck contents.

S: Fifty-five dollars?

J: Yes, one dollar for each mile above the limit, that makes twenty-five dollars, and thirty dollars for being careless.

S: I should've known better!

J: Yes, you'll have learned a costly lesson. Next case, please.

How's that?: What are you saying?
trap: ambush, catch
warn: give notice
damage: injury, loss of value

contents: the things inside, the amount contained
costly: expensive

Narrative: He Should Have Listened

1. Once upon a time, there was a tiny kingdom. The ruler of that
    kingdom was called *king*. The king was a very powerful person. He
    would always rule alone, and his wishes were obeyed as far and
    wide as you could ride a horse for an entire week. The king sat on a
    throne inside the palace. There he would receive his subjects. From
    the palace he ordered things to be done. The orders of the ruler
    were obeyed to please him. Most people of that time were poor and
    ignorant. Only the king and his helpers were educated. That was
    long, long ago.

2. As time went on, the old king died and a new ruler took over. Not
    much would change with the new king. He, too, would sit on his
    throne and order things to be done. On and on it would happen
    that when a king would die, another ruler would continue to rule
    the same old way.

3. One day, a wise old man came to visit the tiny kingdom. He would
    walk each day to the marketplace. On his way he would see the
    poverty and talk with the people. He saw how ignorant the people
    were and decided to use his time to educate them as best he could.

---

tiny: very small
ruler: dictator
king: monarch
powerful: strong, mighty
rule: govern, dictate
entire: whole
throne: royal chair
palace: castle; large
  fortified building

subjects: people under the
  authority or control of a ruler
ignorant: uneducated
take over: to manage, rule
on and on: continuously, always
marketplace: where things are sold
poverty: need
decided: determined

4. And one day, the old "wise one," as the people called him, suddenly disappeared. The people wondered where he'd gone. Why would he leave without saying good-bye? But they kept right on learning. And they began looking at things in a way different from before. And much time had passed.

5. Soon, a new king became the ruler of the tiny kingdom. He was evil and ambitious and demanded more than any ruler before him. The people rebelled because they couldn't agree with his ways. But the king wouldn't give in. There was a confrontation.

    The king yelled at his people from the balcony, "You should listen to what I have to say!"

    "Why won't you listen to your people for once?" the people asked their king.

    But the king wouldn't listen to the voices of his people. He wouldn't even listen to his advisers. The people would have none of the king's old ways. They were tired of his ancient rule. They called for a change.

6. The people were still poor, but they were no longer ignorant. They rebelled against the tyranny of the time. They would not love a ruler who wished to keep them ignorant and poor like their ancestors. And there was much noise in the streets of the tiny kingdom.

---

disappear: vanish
wonder: be curious
right on: continued
evil: bad
ambitious: wanting more wealth
demand: want, ask for
rebel: resist
give in: yield, surrender

confrontation: face-to-face challenge
balcony: small platform projecting from a wall of a building
for once: one time
adviser: consultant
none of: no more of
ancient: of times long past, old

If only the ruler would listen! It would not have come to the violence and bloodshed. If only the ambitious king would show some love for his people instead of building castles for himself and his family while the people hungered.

"Why won't the king listen to the voices of his people?" they asked repeatedly.

7. And the king wouldn't listen. He really couldn't come among his people because his pride wouldn't let him do such a thing. Suddenly, it was too late. There was a loud explosion. And then there was silence. It was so quiet that many people said it hurt their ears. The king no longer ruled the little kingdom.

"The king should have paid attention to his people," someone said softly. "All of this bloodshed and fighting wouldn't have happened, but the king wouldn't listen."

8. To this day, the people tell about the lesson they learned from the past. "The king should have learned to change his ways as time went on. If he had, he might still be our leader."

So ends the story of the king who wouldn't hear the cries of his people. They wanted him to govern, but he lived in the past and couldn't see the world changing around him. He only wished to rule.

---

no longer: no more
tyranny: cruel rule
ancestors: forefathers
bloodshed: killing
hunger: have no food
repeatedly: again and again
pride: conceit, exaggerated
  opinion of oneself

explosion: blowup
silence: quiet
ways: customs, how a person
  behaves
leader: one who governs, guides
govern: dictate, rule

VOCABULARY

Dialogue Completion

Fill in the missing word in each of the blank spaces of the dialogue. Select the proper word from the words listed below. One word may be used more than once. Repeat the sentences aloud for correct pronunciation.

costly	zone	traffic signs
fast	guilt	attention
known	consider	paid
mile	court	interrupt
lot	accident	exceeded
time	caused	daydreaming
driving	careful	obey

JUDGE: All motorists know that they must _____ the speed limits. You must have been _____ when you _____ yours.

SUE: But, your honor, I . . .

JUDGE: You should not _____ while I speak, young lady.

SUE: Yes, your honor.

JUDGE: As I said, you should have _____ more _____ to the road and the _____ _____ .

SUE: I know I should have been more _____ . I could have _____ an _____ .

JUDGE: The _____ will _____ your admission of _____ .

SUE: I'll be more _____ in the future. I'm sorry.

JUDGE: I wouldn't be in a hurry _____ through a school _____ .

SUE: I promise I won't, your honor.

JUDGE: The _____ will be twenty-five dollars.

SUE: That's a _____ of money, your honor.

JUDGE: It's one dollar for each _____ exceeding the limit.

SUE: I should have _____ !

JUDGE: Driving too _____ may be very _____ .

Narrative Completion

Fill in each blank space in the text from the list of words preceding each paragraph. A selection may be used more than once, and more than one word may be used in one blank space.

done	rule	ignorant	subjects
powerful	helpers	throne	king
orders	obeyed	ruler	kingdom

1. Once upon a time there was a tiny _____ . The _____
   of that _____ was called _____ . He was a _____
   person. He would always _____ alone. His wishes were
   _____ . The king sat on a _____ inside the palace.
   There he received his _____ . From the _____ he
   ordered things to be _____ . The king's _____ were
   _____ . The people of the tiny _____ were poor and
   _____ . Only the king and his _____ were educated.

continue	order	happen	
change	throne	took	king

2. As time went on, the old _____ died. A new ruler
   _____ over. Not much could _____ with the new
   _____ . He, too, would sit on his _____ and
   _____ things to be done. On and on, it would _____ ,
   when a _____ would die, another ruler would _____
   to rule the same old way.

could   talk   walk   educate
poverty   wise   decided   marketplace
ignorant   people

3. A _____ old man came to visit the tiny kingdom. He would
    _____ down each day to the _____ . On his way he
    would see the _____ , and he would _____ with the
    _____ . He saw how _____ the people were and
    _____ to use his time to _____ them as best he
    _____ .

different   learning   gone   disappeared
looking   saying   wondered   people

4. And one day, the old "wise one," as the _____ called him,
    suddenly _____ . The people _____ where he'd
    _____ . Why would he leave without _____ good-bye?
    But they kept right on _____ . And they began _____
    at things in a way _____ from before.

change   give in   demanded   ancient
agree   ambitious   tired   rebelled
evil   listen   ruler

5. One day, a new king became the _____ . He was _____
    and _____ and _____ more than the previous rulers.
    The people _____ because they couldn't _____ with
    his ways. But the king wouldn't _____ . They asked him to
    _____ to them, but the king wouldn't _____ . The
    people were _____ of his _____ rule. They called for a
    _____ .

family	keep	rebelled	ambitious
ruler	ignorant	noise	tyranny
poor	ancestors	castles	

6. The people were still _____ , but they were no longer
   _____ . They _____ against the _____ of the
   time. They would not have a _____ who wished to
   _____ them _____ and _____ like their
   _____ . And there was much _____ on the streets.
   The _____ king continued to build _____ for himself
   and his _____ .

silence	late	pride	explosion
suddenly	wouldn't	among	

7. The king _____ listen. He really couldn't come _____
   his people because his _____ wouldn't let him do such a
   thing. _____ it was too _____ . There was a loud
   _____ and then there was _____ .

rule	cries	change	lesson
world	story	learned	day
govern	leader	past	

8. To this _____ , the people tell the _____ they learned
   from the _____ . "The king should have _____ to
   _____ his ways as time went on. If he had, he might still be
   our _____ ." So ends the _____ of the king who would-
   n't hear the _____ of his people. They wanted him to
   _____ , but he lived in the _____ and couldn't see the
   changing around him. He only wished to _____ .

VOCABULARLY SUBSTITUTION

Dialogue Completion

Fill in the missing word in each of the blank spaces of the dialogue. Select the proper word or phrase from the words listed below. Read the sentences aloud. (Pedro = P, Clarissa = C)

expensive   confession   having pleasant thoughts
cautious   follow   velocity
went beyond   drivers   keep in mind
area   road signals   mishap
give   ambush   notice

P: All _____ know that they must _____ the _____ limits. You must have been _____ when you _____ .

C: I didn't see the _____ _____ .

P: You could have caused a _____ .

C: I hope the court will _____ my _____ of guilt.

P: You should be more _____ next time.

C: Yes, especially in the school _____ .

P: That's when the police set up the speed _____ .

C: And they don't _____ you _____ lessons.

P: You can't afford such _____ lessons.

C: I sure can't.

Narrative Completion

Fill in the proper form of the missing word in the blank space of the narrative. Select the word from the words listed preceding each paragraph below. One word may be used more than once. Read sentences aloud.

mighty	monarch	royal chair
dictator	followed	very small	govern

1. Once upon a time, there was a _____ kingdom. The _____ of that kingdom was called _____ . He was a very _____ person. He would always _____ alone. He sat on a _____ , and everybody _____ him.

dictator	would rule	always	continuously
uneducated			

2. The people in the kingdom were poor and _____ . One day, another king _____ _____ . Things didn't change. _____ , as it did before, it would happen that when a king would die, another _____ would continue.

determined	where things are sold	every
great need	very small	

3. A wise old man came to visit the _____ kingdom. He would walk _____ day to the place _____ . On his way he would see _____ and talk with the people. He _____ that he would educate the people.

vanished	were curious	continued	started

4. One day, the old "wise one" suddenly _____ . The people _____ _____ about where he'd gone. But they _____ learning. And they _____ looking at things in a different way.

old   resisted   very small   consultants
wanted   dictator   one time   wanted more weath
monarch   yield   bad

5. Soon, a new _____ became the _____ of the _____
    kingdom. He was _____ and _____ _____
    _____ . He _____ more than any _____ before
    him. The people _____ . But the _____ would not
    _____ . _____ _____ he wouldn't even listen to
    his _____ . People were tired of his _____ rule.

uneducated   resisted   dictator   no more

6. The people were still poor, but they were _____ _____
    ignorant. They _____ the tyranny of the time. They would
    not have a _____ who wished to keep them _____ and
    poor like their ancestors.

killing   blowup   quiet   conceit

7. The king would not listen in his _____ . He couldn't come
    among his people because his _____ wouldn't let him.
    Suddenly, it was too late. There was a loud _____ . And then
    there was _____ . "All of this _____ was unnecessary,"
    the people said. "The king should have listened."

dictate   monarch   learned   altered
one who governs   speak   his customs   changing

8. To this day, the people _____ about the lesson they
    _____ from the past. "The king should have changed
    _____ _____ . If he had, he might still be the
    _____ _____ _____ ." So ends the story of the
    _____ who wouldn't hear the cries of his people. They want-
    ed him to be _____ , but he lived in the past and couldn't see
    the world _____ around him. He only wished to _____ .

PICTOGRAPHS (WORDS IN CONTEXT)

Below are some drawings based on the dialogue presentation. Use the words or phrases listed under each drawing to compose your own dialogue in the first (I) person. A word may be used more than once. In addition to those given here, words of your own choosing may be used.

Active vocabulary: motorists, obey, speed limits, interrupt, your honor, young lady, paid attention, more careful, courtroom, pay attention

Active vocabulary: speed traps, careful, damages, truck contents, drive faster, caught, warned, each mile, careless, costly lesson, accident, truck, melons

Below are some drawings based on the narrative presentation. Use the words or phrases listed below each drawing to construct a short narrative of your own. Words may be used repeatedly. In addition to those listed here, words of your own choosing may be used.

Active vocabulary for paragraphs 1, 2 and 3: king, kingdom, powerful, wishes obeyed, sat on throne, received subjects, palace, poor and ignorant, helpers educated, died, another ruler, took over, order things done, on and on, wise man, poverty, decided to educate

Active vocabulary for paragraphs 4, 5, and 6: wise one, disappeared, wandered, would leave, began looking, different way, time passed, new king, ambitious, evil, demanded, rebelled, couldn't agree, give in, balcony, wouldn't listen, called for a change, no longer ignorant, tyranny, like their ancestors, violence and bloodshed

Active vocabulary from paragraphs 7 and 8: wouldn't listen, pride, suddenly, too late, loud explosion, silence, quiet, paid attention, fighting, lesson, past, leader, king wouldn't hear, govern, wanted to rule

Crossword Puzzle

The puzzle below is based on the dialogue presentation. First, fill in the missing words in the sentences, then write them in the puzzle.

1. All motorists must _____ speed limits.
2. Pay _____ to the road when you drive.
3. Look at the _____ signs.
4. I should have been more _____ .
5. You could have caused an _____ .
6. The _____ will be kind to you.
7. I wouldn't be in a hurry when _____ .
8. You'll get a _____ fine.
9. This was a speed _____ .
10. I have learned a _____ lesson.

GRAMMAR

Explanation and Examples

Here we continue the discussion concerning the use of *modal auxiliaries,* now mostly in their **perfect** tenses. When used in the perfect tense, modals assume different meanings and inferences (conclusions).

The function of **perfect modals** as expressed in their **meaning** (semantics) may be summarized into six different categories: **advisability, conditioned result, inferred certainty, inferred probability, possibility,** and **prediction.** All of the above categories seem to stress the **unreal, hypothetical** (maybe) aspect rather than the **real.** (We will learn more about that when we discuss the *conditional* in Chapters 7 and 8.) Remember that there are not as many meanings for the perfect modals as there are for the simple modals (Chapter 5). The meanings of most simple modals do not carry over into the perfect tense.

<u>*Advisability*</u>	— advice given too late to be of any use
should have .	You **should have** been more careful.
	He **should have** paid attention.
shouldn't have	He **shouldn't have** driven so fast.
	She **shouldn't have** been daydreaming.
might have	At least they **might have** warned me.
	At least my friends **might have** come with me.
could have	At least he **could have** given me a lower fine.
	At least they **could have** sent their good wishes.
<u>*Conditioned result*</u>	— expressing a condition **contrary** to fact
would have	Max **would have** told me about the speed trap if he had known I was going that way.
	He **would have** come with me if he had heard that I needed him.

could have	I **could have** avoided the ticket if I'd known about the speed trap.
	The judge **could have** punished me if I'd lied about it.

Inferred certainty	— **must** in the perfect tells us that we can believe something happened; **can't** infers the opposite
must have	You **must have** been speeding.
	The police **must have** been telling the truth.
can't have	You **can't have** done that already.
	She **can't have** told the whole story.

Inferred probability	— expresses expectation of facts on the part of the speaker; the **outcome** of the expectation may or may not be known
should have	They **should have** found the stolen car by now (though we don't know if they have).
	They **should have** caught you long ago (though for some reason they didn't).

Possibility	— a person has the **ability** to do something or make something happen
may have	Your friend **may have** been lying.
	The police **may have** told the truth.
might have	The police **might have** been hiding the speed trap.
	The judge **might have** already seen the police report.
could have	They **could have** seen another car.
	You **could have** received another fine.
can have	Anna is late. What **can have** happened to her?
	Sue got a traffic ticket. What **can have** been on her mind while driving?

<u>*Prediction*</u>	— indicates an event in the **future time**
will have	When I'm through with you, you **will have** learned a lesson.
	By tomorrow morning I **will have** read the book.
shall have	By next month I **shall have** repaid my debts.
(use only in the first person singular (I) and plural (we)	By next year we **shall have** passed new traffic laws.

Practice

Identify in the following sentences the *modal auxiliary* and the **function** for which it is used.

Example: You should have been more careful.   _____*should have*_____
                                                                    advisability

1. He should have paid attention.   _____

2. At least he could have given me a lower fine. _____

3. At least my friends might have come with me. _____

4. I would have told you about the speed trap
    if I had known about it.   _____

5. We could have avoided the traffic if the
    radio had warned us.   _____

6. You must have been speeding.   _____

7. You can't have done that already.   _____

8. My friend may have told a lie.   _____

9. They could have seen another car.   _____

10. What can have happened to Anna?   _____

11. The judge might have already seen it.   _____

Below are sentences with the modals left out. Write the modals in the blank spaces and identify their function. After completing all of the sentences, check the answers that follow the exercise.

Example: Joe got an *F* in math. He __**should**__ have studied harder.
        advisability

1. By next week I _____ have learned the lesson.

2. You _____ have paid more attention to the road.

3. I _____ not have gotten the ticket.

4. At least you _____ have slowed down.

5. At least he _____ have given me a lower fine.

6. What _____ have happened to Anna?

7. When the time comes, I _____ have read the book.

8. They _____ have followed another car.

9. Your friend _____ have been right.

10. My friend _____ 't have done that already.

(Answers to the above exercise: 1. **will** = prediction; 2. should = advisability; 3. would = conditioned result; 4. might = advisability; 5. could = advisability; 6. can = possibility; 7. **will** = prediction; 8. could = possibility; 9. may = possibility; 10. can = inferred certainty

IDEA RECOGNITION

Copy from the model narrative sentences telling:

1. What the ruler of the kingdom was called

_____

2. How the ruler was

_____

3. How he would always rule

_____

4. What happened to his wishes

_____

5. Where the king sat

_____

6. Who the poor and ignorant were

_____

7. Who the educated were

_____

8. Who followed the king to the throne

_____

9. How the next ruler would continue

_____

10. Who came to visit the kingdom

_____

11. What the wise man did

_____

12. How the new ruler was

_____

13. Why he wouldn't listen to his people

_____

14. What the people were tired of

_____

15. Why they rebelled

_____

16. What happened in the streets

_____

17. Why the king couldn't come among his people

_____

18. What suddenly happened

_____

19. What the people tell about to this day

_____

20. What the people wanted

_____

21. What the king wanted

_____

VOCABULARY ENRICHMENT

Following are paraphrases of expressions or words from the model narrative. Find those expressions and write them on the blank lines below. Repeat the expressions aloud.

Example: a long time ago = **once upon a time**

1. a. There was a very small monarchy

    _____

    b. The monarch was mighty

    _____

    c. He sat on a royal chair

    _____

    d. His people were told to do things

    _____

e. The monarch and his aide were literate

_____

2. a. In the course of time

_____

b. There were no changes

_____

c. Continuously

_____

3. a. The old man saw the need of the people

_____

b. He communicated with the people

_____

c. He made up his mind to teach them.

_____

4. a. One day the old man was no longer there

_____

b. The people were curious

_____

c. They continued learning

_____

5. a. Wanted more wealth

_____

b. He wanted more than the past rulers

_____

    c.   People resisted but the king wouldn't yield

    d.   They did not like his rule of times long past

6.   a.   The people were no longer uneducated

    b.   They wouldn't remain like their forefathers

    c.   There was much killing

    d.   The people had no food

7.   a.   His conceit did not allow him to listen

    b.   It came to a blowup

8.   a.   To the present

    b.   He should not have remained the way he was

    c.   He should have guided his people

    d.   The king wanted to dictate

Conceptualizations

Sometimes we give or receive advice about an event in the past. This advice is too late, because what has happened has already happened. We use **should have** when we talk about something we wish we (or someone) had done but didn't do. Make up your own **modal** sentences for the situations described following each set of examples.

Examples:

Eduardo got a speeding ticket. He didn't pay attention. He **should have** paid attention.

Raul drove very fast. He had an accident. He shouldn't have driven so fast.

1. Sue had an accident. She was not careful.

_____

2. This morning I was late for school. I didn't set my alarm clock.

_____

3. Gregory drove his car into a ditch. He was daydreaming and didn't notice the ditch was there.

_____

4. We all know that speed limits must be observed. Sue was careless and drove fifty miles in a thirty mile per hour zone. Sue had to appear in court.

_____

Below are some statements about different people. Read them carefully, then tell what these people should have done, or shouldn't have done.

1. Bill told his friend about Sue's accident. This was not a nice thing to do.

   _____

2. Joan left her purse on her desk yesterday. When she returned to look for it, it was gone.

   _____

3. Sue's car was stolen last month. She was told to lock it, but she didn't take time to do it.

   _____

4. My little sister got a stomachache from eating too many apples. She was told not to overeat, but she did anyway.

   _____

5. Mary Lou failed her exams. She was told to study for her exams, but instead of studying she went to the movies with Gregory.

   _____

Sometimes we guess about past happenings, even when we are not at all certain about what happened. In such cases we say something **could** (or **may**) have happened, or, if there is little chance for it to happen, it **might have** happened.

Examples: Yvonne was supposed to study with me last night, but she didn't come. I don't know what happened.

She **could have** forgotten. She **may have tried** to call. She **might have phoned** when I was out.

Guess what happened in the following examples:

1. My friend was angry last night. What do you suppose the matter was?

   _____

   _____

2. Josef planned to come by last weekend, but he didn't.
   Do you know why?

   _____

   _____

3. Sue's friends wanted to warn her about the speed trap, but they didn't. Why do you suppose they kept it from her?

_____

_____

4. I left my office and stopped for a cup of coffee at a sidewalk cafe. When I got home, I noticed that my housekeys were gone. What do you think happened?

_____

_____

5. Mark and Louisa planned to take a motorcycle ride into the country. No sooner were they out of the city when the motorcycle came to a halt. What do you suppose was the cause?

_____

_____

STEPS IN CREATIVE EXPRESSION

Write the modal perfects on the line. Read them aloud and identify the function of the modals. Then write your own sentence using the same modal perfect and performing the same function. Read the sentences aloud.

1. She **should have** called.

_____

2. Joe **could have** come.

_____

3. Jenny **might have** called.

_____

4. Fritz **may have** been here.

_____

5. At least they **might have** told me.

_____

6. At least they **could have** sent their wishes.

_____

7. Max **would have** told me about it if he had known.

_____

8. You **can't have** done that already.

_____

9. She **can't have** told the whole story.

_____

10. They **should have** caught the thief by now.

_____

11. Your friend **may** have been telling the truth.

_____

12. You **could have** seen another car.

_____

13. Anna is late. What **can have** happened to her?

_____

14. By next week you **will** have learned your lesson.

_____

15. By next year we **shall have** passed new laws.

_____

Below is the scene of a big accident. There is a train, two cars, and a taxi cab at a railroad crossing. There is also a big truck which is used to carry fruit to the market. The truck is damaged and the fruit scatters on the road and railroad crossing. Both cars are badly damaged, and the taxi cab has a broken fender. Now, you are the sheriffs deputy. Try to guess how this accident might have happened by looking at the circumstances.

1. What must have happened first?

_____

2. Could the taxi have traveled too fast?

_____

3. Could the truck have spilled the fruit and made the train stop suddenly?

_____

4. How could the taxi's fender have been damaged?

_____

5. Could the truck have been in bad condition?

_____

6. Could the first car have come to a sudden stop?

_____

7. Could the train have stopped without signaling?

_____

8. Could the crossing signals have been out of order?

_____

9. What must have happened when the signals didn't work?

_____

Create a dialogue similar to the model presentation based on the expressions below. Read the sentences aloud. (Bob = B, Attorney = A)

A: Motorists know _____ obey limit _____ .

B: But _____ speed trap _____ .

A: _____ too fast _____ important _____ .

B: _____ sorry. _____ didn't pay attention _____ .

A: _____ should watch _____ all traffic _____ .

B: _____ first accident _____ .

A: I know _____ everyone says _____ .

B: Sue _____ should have known _____ .

A: The court _____ consider _____ guilt _____ .

B: _____ should have been _____ careful _____ .

A: I wouldn't have _____ in a hurry _____ .

B: _____ I'll have learned _____ lesson _____ .

A: That might be _____ .

Vignette

Read carefully and learn the new words and facts. Discuss them in the classroom.

The Statue of Liberty

1. Probably the most popular sight to visit in New York City is the Statue of Liberty. When you arrive in New York City by ship, you pass the statue which stands on an island near the city. The statue welcomes all travelers coming to the United States.

2. The Statue of Liberty was made in France. It is a gift from the French people to the people of America. The statue is a woman. She holds a torch up high in her right hand. In her left hand she holds a book of law. The torch is a light which shows all ships the way to freedom in America. The law book means that there is also freedom in the law.

3. The statue is very large, and people can walk inside it. People can walk up to the head of the statue. There, they can stand and look out to see the passing ships and the ocean. When the weather is good and the day is clear you can see for many miles around.

---

popular: what people like
sight: something to see
liberty: freedom
statue: sculpture, work of art
welcome: greet

gift: present
torch: a burning light
base: foundation, support
stand for: mean, signify

4. At the base of the statue, there is a short poem written by Emma Lazarus. It begins with the words "Give me your poor," and it continues with words welcoming all people who come to America.

5. For many years the Statue of Liberty has become known to all people. It stands for freedom and liberty for all people. It means love and peace to all who know its story. The French people gave it to the Americans. The American children gave money to build the foundation on which the statue now stands. Each gave with love. This is why the statue means love, peace, and understanding among all people.

You visited the Statue of Liberty. Now, tell the class about your experience. You can talk about the following:

1. a. When the Statue of Liberty is seen
   b. Where it stands
   c. What it does

2. a. Who made the statue
   b. How it came to America
   c. What the statue is
   d. How the statue holds the torch
   e. What the statue shows
   f. What the statue holds in her left hand
   g. What the book of law means

3. a. Where the people can walk
   b. What the people can see
   c. When the people can see for many miles around

4. a. What can be found at the base of the statue
   b. Who wrote the poem
   c. How the poem begins
   d. What the poem does

5. a. Who knows the statue
   b. Who gave it to America
   c. Who gave money for the foundation
   d. What the statue stands for

COMMENTARY ON MODEL PRESENTATIONS

Here are some points of information. Tell what must have happened.
Use modal perfects in your responses. Read the sentences aloud.

FREE COMPOSITION

1. There is broken glass on the street at the railroad crossing.

   _____

   _____

2. Sue stands next to her damaged car. She is very worried.

   _____

   _____

3. People are standing around. The police and an ambulance have
   arrived.

   _____

   _____

4. Sue is standing in front of the judge.

   _____

   _____

5. Sue's husband is waiting for her at home, but Sue is late.

   _____

   _____

6. Sue is crying because she has to pay a traffic fine.

_____

_____

7. The judge admonishes Sue for speeding.

_____

_____

8. Sue admits her guilt.

_____

_____

9. She regrets her friends didn't tell her about the speed trap.

_____

_____

10. The judge is angry with Sue.

_____

_____

FREE COMPOSITION

Dialogue Improvisation

Compose your own dialogue, using the situation given below. Read the dialogue aloud.

1. You are late for an appointment.
2. You ask a friend to take you there.
3. Your friend regrets that you call late and he has another task to do.
4. You ask for the telephone number to call a taxi.
5. You tell the taxi driver to take you there.

6. The taxi driver does not know the way.

7. You tell him he should have brought a city map.

8. He replies that he had not driven in that section of town.

9. You tell him that he must know his way as a taxi driver.

Fill in the Missing Dialogue

For each of the drawings below, write your own dialogue which describes the action.

Compose a short narrative, building on the expressions below.

1. . . . upon a time . . . of that kingdom . . . rule alone . . . the orders . . . obeyed . . .

2. . . . time went on . . . not much would change . . . would sit on his throne . . . the same old way.

3. . . . the tiny kingdom . . . would walk . . . ignorant. . . people . . . as best he could.

4. . . . "wise one" . . . kept right on . . . time passed.

5. . . . became the ruler . . . evil and ambitious . . . The people . . . "should listen". . . but the king wouldn't listen . . . a change.

6. . . . no longer ignorant. . . . against the tyranny . . . wished . . . like ancestors . . . castles for himself . . . they asked. . . .

7. . . . his pride . . . there was. . . explosion . . .. silence . . . bloodshed and fighting . . .

8. to this day . . . should have learned . . . king wouldn't hear . . . lived in the past. . . . world changing . . . he only wished . . .

CHAPTER SEVEN

If You're So Smart, Why Aren't You Rich?
Supposing

IN THIS CHAPTER

Words to Remember

The Conditional		*Verb Form Used*
Neutral *conditional*	=	*"if"* + **Present**
Wish *sentence* (*Present Time*)	=	**Past**
Future *time* condition with *"if"*	=	**Present**

provided (that) or providing (that), in the event that, whether. . . or (whether)

MODEL PRESENTATION

Dialogue: If You 're so Smart, Why Aren't You Rich?

(Teacher = T, Maria = M, Gloria = G, Itaka = I)

T: Students, today we'll begin to study our solar system.

M: What's a solar system?

I: Don't you know? It consists of the sun, the stars and the moon and the other bodies that revolve around the sun.

G: And the planets, too?

T: Yes, the planets too. If we all listen attentively, we'll probably know much more about this interesting subject.

I: Do you think the other planets are inhabited like the earth?

T: This is what science is trying to determine right now.

G: If the planets are inhabited, the inhabitants are probably different from us.

T: What makes you think so?

G: Well, if we travel to foreign countries, we can notice differences among people.

M: Yes, just imagine traveling as far as the planet Mars or Mercury. Isn't that strange?

I: I'll be happy to go provided I can return to earth.

G: Why do you make conditions like that? Do you really like it on earth so much?

I: Whether I like it here on earth or whether I like it on Mars, I want to return to the place of my birth.

---

solar system: the sun and all the heavenly bodies

planet: celestial body

attentively: thoughtfully paying attention

subject: topic

inhabited: lived in

determine: find out, discover

different: not alike, distinct

difference: dissimilarity

imagine: visualize

strange: unusual

provided: if

true: faithful

T: Spoken like a true son of the earth.

M: I really don't know. In the event that I am selected to explore a planet, I'll make up my mind about staying there after I examine it carefully.

T: Why not study all about it before the trip?

M: It's more fun learning from experience.

I: Tell us more about it, teacher. We want to be prepared.

T: What do you wish for most at this very moment?

G: We wish we understood more about the planets.

M: No, no. We wish we had a lot of money.

T: What for?

M: To go visit the stars.

I: Wouldn't it be wonderful?

T: We can learn much from just reading about it, can't we? Would you have the courage to travel into space?

M: I believe I would.

I: When I was small, I once read Jules Verne's *Journey to the Center of the Earth*. I wouldn't have missed it for anything.

T: You see? We can all learn from the experiences of others.

G: But that was fantasy!

T: Fantasy or not, much truth can be found in it.

I: If we read more about it, we would be better prepared.

G: Sure. If we lived in Africa, we would know a lot about its people.

T: There is no limit to learning. Knowledge is a cumulative process, which means that if we remember what we learned yesterday, we can add to it today and tomorrow, etc.

M: You know so much, teacher.

G: But, if you're so smart, teacher, why aren't you rich?

---

select: choose

explore: search, investigate

examine: study

experience: personal involvement

prepare: arrange, make ready

at this very moment: right now

courage: bravery, valor

fantasy: imagination

limit: end

cumulative: progressive addition

process: system

smart: wise

Narrative: Supposing

1. It is written that once God told King Solomon to make three important wishes. To that King Solomon replied: "Give me good health, good luck, and wisdom." It is also written that God granted those three wishes to King Solomon, and the famous king lived a long, happy, and prosperous life. His wisdom was known throughout the land.

2. Let's suppose that if someone tells you that you may make a wish, you will probably ask for something that you like. If your parents are wealthy, you will probably ask for a big car. If your parents are not rich, you will want a lot of money. If you have the money, you might be happy. That's what you think.

3. However, money does not always bring happiness. If you become very rich, the news media will announce it to the whole world. Soon you'll be afraid to leave your home because thieves might break in when you are gone. Being wealthy and having material possessions does not guarantee happiness. You will have no trouble with it, provided you lead a quiet and unpretentious life.

4. Oftentimes, we wish we had many things that we don't really need. That's how people are. When we understand life only a little, we wish we understood it more. We know English pretty well now. We wish we knew it better. It's like that with most people. When they have something, they always wish they had more of it. That's what we call "human nature."

---

supposing: imagining
reply: answer
wisdom: intelligence, good judgment
grant: give
prosperous: rich, well-to-do
throughout: all through

probably: likely **wealthy:** rich
news media: radio, newspapers, etc.
break in: burglarize, rob
gone: away
material: physical
possessions: belongings
guarantee: ensure

5. It is safe to assume that persons who always want more than they possess will remain unhappy. If they lived in a small house, they would want it to be bigger. If they had a bigger house, they would want some fancy furniture. If they didn't have a big car, they would want one. This can go on and on and on.

6. Persons who are happy with themselves are generally happy with the world. If they had a big home, they would be satisfied. If they didn't have a big home, they would also be contented. Happiness depends on the way we see the world. If we didn't look at our world with gratitude for all the things we have, we would remain forever unhappy. Supposing you had all you wished for, would you wish for more?

Dialogue Completion

Fill in the missing word in each of the blank spaces of the dialogue. Select the proper word from the words listed below. One word may be used more than once. Repeat the sentences aloud for correct pronunciation.

space	select	space	fantasy
explore	subject	prepare	strange
attentive	experience	solar system	planets
imagined			

JOSHUA: Hi, Tamara. I haven't seen you for quite some time. What have you been doing?

TAMARA: Studying the _____ _____ .

JOSHUA: The _____ _____ ? What's that?

---

unpretentious: simple
oftentimes: many times
pretty: quite
human nature: the way people are
safe: secure
assume: suppose

remain: stay
fancy: extravagant
generally: usually
satisfied: contented
depend (on): rely (on)
gratitude: thankfulness

TAMARA: You know, everything about the _____ .

JOSHUA: Go on, go on, tell me more.

TAMARA: You'd have to be really _____ . I wouldn't want to waste my time.

JOSHUA: Honestly, I'd love to learn more about that _____ . I've always _____ all kinds of _____ things about the _____ _____ .

TAMARA: They're not _____ at all. Scientists are just now beginning to _____ the _____ _____ .

JOSHUA: Next semester, I'll _____ this _____ . I'd love to learn from _____ so that I can better _____ to travel into _____ .

TAMARA: Stop joking. This is not a _____ . It's all true. There are many _____ in our _____ _____ .

JOSHUA: I'm not joking. I'm smiling because I'm happy to learn. Knowledge is _____ , you know.

Narrative Completion

Fill in each blank space in the text from the list of words and phrases preceding each paragraph. A selection may be used more than once, and more than one word may be used in one blank space. Read the sentences aloud.

throughout	wisdom	replied	properous
luck	make	granted	health
written	wishes		

1. It is _____ that once God told King Solomon to _____ three important _____ . King Solomon _____ : "Give me good _____ , good _____ and _____ ." God _____ those three _____ to King Solomon. The king lived a long, happy, and _____ life. His _____ was known _____ the land.

might	like	may	will
probably	someone	wealthy	wish
suppose			

2. Let's, _____ that if _____ tells you that you
   _____ make a _____ , you will _____ ask for
   something that you _____ . If your parents are _____ ,
   you will _____ for a big car. If your paents are not rich, you
   _____ want a lot of money. If you have the money, you
   _____ be happy.

unpretentious	material	whole	provided
media	break in	trouble	home
happiness	guarantee		

3. However, money does not always bring _____ . If you
   become very rich, the news _____ will announce it to the
   _____ world. Soon you'll be afraid to leave your _____
   because thieves might _____ _____ when you are
   gone. Being wealthy and having _____ possessions does not
   _____ you lead an _____ life.

| human nature | little | need | knew |
| people | had | understood | something |

4. Oftentimes, we wish we _____ many things that we don't
   really _____ . That's how _____ are. When we understand life only a _____ , we wish we _____ it more. We
   know English pretty well now. We wish we _____ it better.
   It's like that with most _____ . When they have _____
   they always wish they _____ more of it. That what we call
   " _____ _____ ."

| didn't | possess | had | persons |
| would | assume | lived | fancy |

5. It is safe to _____ that _____ who always want more than they _____ will remain unhappy. If they _____ in a small house, they _____ want it to be bigger. If they _____ a bigger house, they _____ wnat some _____ furniture. If they _____ have a big car, they _____ want one.

wished	didn't	had	generally
gratitude	satisfied	world	themselves
depends	would		

6. Persons who are happy with _____ are _____ happy with the _____ . If they _____ a big house, they _____ be _____ . If they _____ a big home, they _____ also be contented. Happiness _____ on the way we see the _____ . If we _____ look at our _____ with _____ for all the things we have, we _____ remain forever unhappy. Supposing you _____ all you _____ for, _____ you wish for more?

Dialogue Completion

Fill in the missing words in each of the blank spaces of the dialogue. Select the proper word or phrase from the words listed below. Read the sentences aloud. (Annette = A, Jaime = J, Regina = R)

continuous	unusual	dissimilarity	celestial bodies
end	faithful	distinct	topic
personal	if	found out	paying attention
involvement	progressive	lived in	the sun and all
study	visualize		the heavenly bodies

J: Let's talk about the _____ _____ .

A: You mean about the sun and the stars and the moon?

R: Sure, that's what he means.

A: Also, about _____ .

J: Yes, about _____ too. I haven't been _____
_____ during our class period.

R: Neither have I. But I'd love to know more about this interesting

_____ .

A: Do you think the other _____ are _____ like the earth?

R: That hasn't been _____ yet.

A: If they are _____ , the inhabitants are probably from us.

J: What makes you think so?

A: Well, if we travel to a foreign country, we can notice _____
among people.

R: Just _____ traveling to Mars. Isn't that _____ ?

A: I will be happy _____ I can return to earth.

J: Spoken like a _____ daughter of our planet.

R: I will _____ all of the _____ before I undertake the trip.

A: But it's more fun when we learn from _____ .

R: We always wish we understood more about the _____ .

J: Yes, there is no _____ to learning. It's a _____ process.

Narrative Completion

Fill in the missing words in each of the blank spaces of the narrative.
Select the proper word or phrase from the words listed preceding each
paragraph below.

intelligence   given   imagine   well-to-do   answer

1. _____ that you are given three wishes. What will be your
_____ ? If you are _____ what you ask for, what will
you do? Do you like to be _____ ? I know of a person who
only wants _____ to be happy.

rich   likely   father and mother
a person   imagine

2. Let's _____ that _____ tells you that you can make one
wish. You will _____ ask for a big car. But if your
_____ are not _____ , you will ask for a lot of money.

simple   physical   ensure   burglarize

3. Money does not always bring happiness. If you are rich, someone
will _____ your house. Having _____ possessions is
not very important. They don't _____ happiness. It is better
to live a _____ life.

the way people are   quite
persons   many times

4. _____ we wish we had more than we need. When we know
something _____ well, we wish we knew it better. It's like
that with most _____ . That's _____ .

extravagant   suppose   stay   secure

5. It is _____ to _____ that persons who always want
more will _____ unhappy. If they had a big house, they
would want some _____ furniture. This can go on and on.

stay   relies   thankfulness

contented   universe   usually

6. Persons who are unhappy with themselves are unhappy with the world. Those who are _____ with themselves are _____ with others. Happiness _____ on the way we see the _____ . If we didn't look at our _____ with _____ for all the things we have, we would _____ unhappy forever.

PICTOGRAPHS (WORDS IN CONTEXT)

Below are some drawings based on the dialogue presentation. Use the words or phrases listed under each drawing to compose your own dialogue. The same words may be used more than once. In addition to those given here, words of your own choosing may be used.

Active vocabularly: solar system, star, sun, planet, moon, interesting subject

Active vocabularly: inhabited, science, determine, different, inhabitants, foreign country

Active vocabulary: travel, Mars and Mercury, strange, provided, return, place of birth, selected to explore, examine, be prepared, learn from experience, cumulative process

Below are some drawings based on the narrative presentation. Use the words or phrases listed below each drawing to construct a short narrative of your own. Words may be used repeatedly. In addition to those listed here, words of your own choosing may be used.

Active vocabulary from paragraphs 1, 2, 3 and 4: rich, news media, break in, material, possessions, guarantee, happiness, unpretentious, wish, often

Active vocabulary from paragraphs 5 and 6: safe, assume, remain, unhappy, small home, fancy furniture, persons, happy, themselves, generally, satisfied, happiness depends, gratitude, remain, supposing

Crossword Puzzle

The puzzle below is based on the model dialogue presentation. First, fill in the missing words in the sentences, then write them in the puzzle.

1. Today we study our _____ system.
   down
2. It is the study of _____ .
   across
3. That's an interesting _____ .
   down
4. The inhabitants are _____ different.
   across
5. I will be happy _____ I can return.
   across

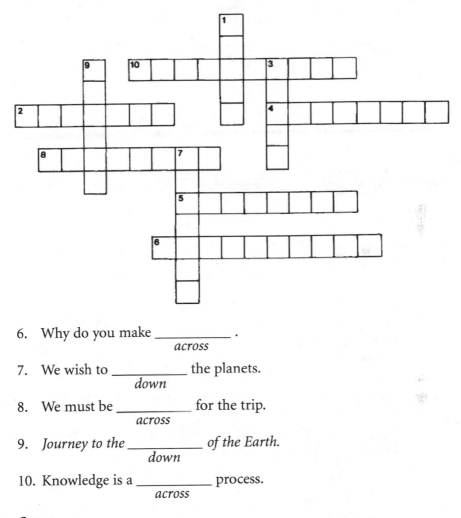

6. Why do you make _____ .
   across

7. We wish to _____ the planets.
   down

8. We must be _____ for the trip.
   across

9. *Journey to the _____ of the Earth.*
   down

10. Knowledge is a _____ process.
    across

Song

Below are the words and music of an old spiritual song. It is called *spiritual* because it expresses the spirit of the people. It gives courage to a person to do what that person thinks is right. This song tells of a purpose in life: to rise above all difficult times and build a better future, a "better world."

We Shall Overcome

We shall o-ver-come, —— we shall o-ver-come, ——

We shall o- ver- come some day. —————————— Oh, ——

deep in my heart I do be- lieve

We shall o- ver- come some day. ——

We shall walk in peace,
We shall walk in peace,
We shall walk in peace some day.
Oh, deep in my heart
I do believe
We shall walk in peace some day.

We shall build a new world,
We shall build a new world,
We shall build a new world some day.
Oh, deep in my heart
I do believe
We shall build a new world some day.

Answer the following questions:

1. What kind of song is a *spiritual* song?
2. What does this song give the people?
3. What does the song tell?
4. How will we walk?
5. What will we build?
6. When will we build a better world?

GRAMMAR

Explanation and Examples

In chapters 5 and 6, we studied the modal auxiliary. We learned about the various functions of the modals, their own meanings, and the meanings they add to the verb-**implying, guessing, hypothesizing, conjecturing,** etc.

In chapters 7 and 8 we will study equally important aspects of the English language: telling the **real** from the **hypothetical, the contrary to fact** as relating to the **possible, the probable, the certain,** and the **future.**

The simplest of the conditional statements is the **neutral conditional** sentence. It uses *if* in the conditional clause plus the **present** tense of the verb. The **main** clause is also in the **present** tense.

Examples: If the planets **are** inhabited, the inhabitants **are** probably different from us.

If we **travel** to a foreign country, we **can** notice differences among people.

If we **reach** the planets, there **are** many surprises for us.

Some conditional sentences are introduced by certain special words. These words are **transitional expressions** and **subordinating conjunctions.***

Examples: I will be happy to go **provided** I can return to earth.

Whether I like it here on earth or **whether** I like it on Mars, I want to return to earth.

Other conditional sentences begin with the subordinating conjunction *if* and continue in the **main** clause with the **future** tense.

Examples: If I'm selected to explore a planet, **I'll** make up my mind about staying there.

If someone tells you that you may make a wish, you **will** probably ask for something that you like.

*See Appendix IV.

If your parents are wealthy, you **will** probably ask for a big car.

If your parents are not rich, you **will** want a lot of money.

If you have the money, you **will** be happy.

Quite often, the conditional takes on the nature of a **wish.** Even though the wish represents a **present** condition, the past form of the verb is used.

Examples: We **wish** we **understood** more about the planets.
We **wish** we **had** a lot of money.

Oftentimes, we **wish** we **had** many things that we don't really need.

We **wish** we **knew** it better.

Also, at times, we can express the **contrary to fact** condition by using a verb in the **past** when referring to a **present** condition. In the main clause we use the modals **would, could, should,** etc.

Examples: If we **lived** in Africa, we **would** know a lot about its people.

If they **lived** in a small house, they **would** want it to be bigger.

If they **didn't** have a big car, they **would** want one.

Practice

Repeat the sample sentences, then substitute the new expression into the sample sentence. Read the sentences aloud.

1. If **the planets** are inhabited, the inhabitants are probably different from us.

   > the stars
   > Mars and Jupiter
   > the strange places
   > the distant countries

2. If we travel to **foreign countries,** we can notice differences among people.

   > big cities
   > unusual places
   > faraway lands
   > remote planets

3. If we reach the **planets,** there are many **surprises** for us.

   > stars   rewards
   > store   things to buy
   > planets Mars and   discoveries
   >   Jupiter

4. I will be happy to go provided **I can return.**

   > we will drive.
   > I will fly.
   > you'll go with me.

5. If I'm selected, I'll **go.**

   > think about it.
   > let you know.
   > write you often.

6. If your parents are rich, you'll want to **buy a car.**

   > travel to Africa.
   > buy a jet.
   > study abroad.

7. If you have the money, you will **be happy.**

                                     give to charity.

                                     help people.

                                     build a library.

8. If we all **listen attentively,** we will probably know much more about this interesting subject.

        learn our lessons

        read more often

        discuss it with friends

        go to the movies

9. If you have the **money,** you will **be happy.**

        car   **visit.**

        time   **travel.**

        patience   **learn.**

10. If we **read** more about it, we would be better prepared.

        talked

        thought

        learned

        studied

11. We wish we **understood** more about the planets.

              knew

              read

              talked

12. We wish we **knew** it better.

              did

              understood

              wrote

13. If we **lived** in Africa, we would **know** a lot about its people.

traveled	**learn**
landed	**talk**
arrived	**discuss**

14. If they lived in a **small house,** they would want it to be **bigger.**

big cottage	**smaller.**
castle	**old.**
beach house	**fancy.**

15. If we didn't feel **gratitude,** we would **remain unhappy.**

good	**remain miserable,**
the urge	**stay in bed.**
ambitious	**be lazy.**

IDEA RECOGNITION

Copy from the model narrative the sentences expressing the following

1. King Solomon's three wishes

   _____

2. What was known throughout the land

   _____

3. What you'll ask for if your parents are wealthy

   _____

4. What you'll want if your parents aren't wealthy

   _____

5. What will happen if you have money

   _____

6. What will happen if you become rich

_____

7. When the thieves might break into your home

_____

8. When you will have no trouble

_____

9. How people are

_____

10. Why we wish we knew everything better

_____

11. How it is with most people

_____

12. What's safe to assume

_____

13. What people would want if they had a bigger house

_____

14. When people are generally happy

_____

15. How people would be contented

_____

16. When we would remain unhappy

_____

17. When we would wish for more

_____

VOCABULAR Y ENRICHMENT

Answer the questions on the basis of the dialogue. Read the sentences aloud.

1. If we listen attentively, what will we know?

   _____

2. If the planets are inhabited, how will the inhabitants probably be?

   _____

3. If we travel to foreign countries, what will we notice?

   _____

4. If Itaka returns to earth, how will he be?

   _____

5. In the event Maria is selected to explore a planet, what will she decide?

   _____

6. If we read more, how would we be?

   _____

7. If we lived in Africa, what would we know?

   _____

8. What can we do, if we remember what we learned yesterday?

   _____

9. If the teacher is so smart, why isn't he rich?

   _____

Ask questions about the expressions and ideas listed below. Then answer, using the **if-clause** and **main clause**. Consult a dictionary if necessary. Read the sentences aloud.

Example: **If we arrived on Mars, what would the inhabitants be called? If we arrived on Mars, the inhabitants would be called Martians.**

on Pluto	in Canada
in Africa	in Mongolia
in a foreign country	in Texas

Ask questions about the activities of the professions listed below, then answer, using both the **if-clause** and **main clause**. Consult a dictionary if needed. Read the sentences aloud.

Example: **What kind of work would you do, if you were surgeons? If we were surgeons, we would perform surgery.**

masons	architects
musicians	archeologists
teachers	diplomats

Ask and answer questions based on the items below. Read the sentences aloud.

Example: **If our relatives were Frenchmen, where would they live? If our relatives were Frenchmen, they'd (would) live in France.**

Iranians	Israelis	Peruvians
Americans	Poles	Mexicans
Egyptians	Canadians	Brazilians

Guess what would happen if things had occurred differently in the following circumstances.

Example: **We're invited to a boat party. But we arrive late and the boat has sailed without us.**
If we arrived in time for the party, we would sail on the boat.

1.   We were careless, and we received a traffic ticket.

_____

2.   We were late, and the party began without us.

_____

3.   We didn't study, and we failed the exam.

_____

4.   We hurried to school, and we forgot our books.

_____

5.   We didn't save money, and now we can't buy the car we need.

_____

Lexical Units

Select the word from the words listed below that best completes each of the sentences. One selection may be used more than once. Read the sentences aloud.

Example: **If we get home early, we watch the news.** Everybody needs to be **informed.**

more	expensive	understood	gratitude
had	knew	didn't	peaceful
unhappy	satisfied	people	would
ask			

1. Someone tells you that you may make a wish. You will probably _____ for something that you like.

2. If your parents are wealthy, you'll probably ask for an _____ car.

3. Being wealthy does not guarantee happiness. Many wealthy persons are _____ .

4. You will have no trouble if you lead an unpretentious life. An unpretentious life is _____ .

5. Oftentimes, we wish we had many things we don't need. That's how _____ are.

6. When we understand life only a little, we wish we _____ more.

7. We know things pretty well, now. We wish we _____ everything better.

8. When we have something, we always wish we _____ more of it.

9. It is safe to assume that persons who always want more than they possess will remain _____ .

10. If they lived in a small house, they _____ want it to be bigger.

11. If they had a big home, they would be _____ .

12. Happiness depends on the way we see the world. If we _____ look at our world with _____ for all things we have, we would remain _____ forever.

13. Supposing you had all you wished for, would you wish for _____ ?

STEPS IN CREATIVE EXPRESSION

Write what kind of *conditional* is expressed in the following sentences. Read the sentences aloud.   *neutral*

Example: If we listen we will probably learn.   _____

1. If the planets are inhabited, the inhabitants are probably different from us. _____

2. If we travel to foreign countries, we can notice differences among people. _____

3. I will be happy to go, provided I can return to earth. _____

4. In the event that I am selected, I'll make up my mind about staying. _____

5. If we read more, we would be better prepared. _____

6. If we remember what we learned yesterday, we can add to it today. _____

7. If someone tells you that you can make a wish, you will probably ask for something that you like. _____

8. If you have money, you will be happy. _____

9. If they didn't have a big car, they would want one. _____

10. If they had a big home, they would be satisfied. _____

Construct **wish** sentences for the sentences given below. Read the sentences aloud.

Example: We don't have a car. (car)
      We wish we had a car.

1. We know a little math. (more)

   _____

2. We have a small house. (bigger)

   _____

3. They have a big dog. (smaller)

   _____

4. They have something nice. (nicer)

   _____

5. We understand life only a little. (more)

   _____

Create a dialogue similar to model presentation based on the expresions below. (Abdul = A, Yukio = Y, Hiromi = H)

A: _____ what's _____ system?

Y: Don't you _____ ? _____ the stars and the moon _____ .

H: _____ the planets _____ ?

A: _____ other planets _____ inhabited _____ .

Y: _____ science _____ determine _____ .

H: If _____ planets _____ probably _____ different _____ .

Y: _____ really like _____ on earth _____ .

A: Whether _____ on earth _____ on Mars _____ I want _____ place of _____ birth.

Vignette

Read carefully and learn new words and facts. Discuss in the classroom.

The Grand Canyon

1. Each year in the state of Arizona, many tourists come to stand at the rim of the Grand Canyon. At the bottom of the canyon flows the Colorado River.

2. There is nothing like that canyon anywhere else in the world. Its geological story and scenery goes back 1.5 billion years. The rock foundations have many different layers and colors. Each layer took more than 170 million years to be formed.

3. There are many beautiful and interesting sights. One of the most beautiful sights is Supi, the remote village of the Havasupi Indians. The Havasupis inhabit the valley at the western end of the Grand Canyon. They live among beautiful streams, waterfalls, green fields, and ruby-colored walls. Many people who have seen it call this canyon America's Shangri-la—a place to completely get away from the mechanized world in which we live.

Discussion questions

1. a. Where is the Grand Canyon located?
    b. Where do the tourists stand?
    c. What river flows at the bottom of the canyon?

2. a. Is there another such canyon anywhere?
    b. How many years did it take to form?
    c. Describe the rock foundations.

---

rim: edge
bottom: lowest point
canyon: narrow valley between high cliffs
geological: earth science
scenery: view
foundation: base
layer: single thickness lying over or under another
form: create
sight: view
remote: distant, far away
stream: body of running water
waterfall: falling water
ruby-colored: red

3. a. What kind of sights are there?
   b. Who lives in the Supi village?
   c. Is the village easy to reach?
   d. What part of the canyon do the Havasupi Indians inhabit?
   e. Describe the sights among which the Havasupis live.
   f. Why is the remote village of the Havasupis called Shangri-la?

COMMENTARY ON MODEL PRESENTATION

Using key words and phrases from the model narrative, comment on the topics presented below.

supposing	probably	understand	wishes
wealthy	want more	reply	big car
assume	health	happy	remain
luck	material	fancy	wisdom
possessions	generally	grant	guarantee
satisfied	prosperous	unpretentious	depend on
throughout	happiness	gratitude	forever

1. a. Tell what is most important in your life.
   b. If you were given three wishes, what should you wish for?
   c. Comment on what would make you happy: new car, big house, good health, success, etc.

2. a. Discuss the points in the model narrative that impressed you the most.
   b. Discuss the points in the model narrative that impressed you the most.
   c. Give an appropriate title to your composition.

FREE COMPOSITION

Dialogue Improvisation

Compose your own dialogue, using the situation given below. Read the dialogue aloud.

1. You are with a group of your friends.
2. One person suggests talking about the solar system.
3. You ask what it is.
4. Another person explains the solar system.
5. You say you'd like to explore the planets.
6. Someone says that we know very little about the solar system.
7. Another person says that scientists are now investigating the planets.

Fill in the Missing Dialogue

For each of the drawings below, write your own dialogue which describes the action.

Compose a short narrative, building on the expressions given below.

1. ... written ... God told King Solomon ... Solomon replied: " ... good health," etc. ... also written ... king lived a long, happy life.

2. let's... someone tells you ... make a wish. ... If your parents ... wealthy ... what you think.

3. ... money ... bring happiness ... if you become ... rich ... news media ... announce ... soon ... afraid to leave ... thieves break in ... wealthy ... does not guarantee ... will have trouble ... provided ...quiet and unpretentious ...

4. oftentimes, we wish ... don't need ... how people are ... when we understand... we wish ... English pretty well ... we wish ... everything. ...

5. It is safe to assume ... more than ... lived in a small house, they ... bigger ... if had a bigger house, they ... furniture ... didn't have a big car, they. ...

6. persons who are happy ... happy with the world. Happiness depends ... way we see ... If we didn't look ... with gratitude ... would remain forever unhappy.

CHAPTER EIGHT

Would That I Were

Then Why Do We Have Wars?

MODEL PRESENTATION

Dialogue: Would that I Were

(Allan = A, Bette = B)

A: Every time I turn around, there's someone who knows more than I do. I envy such people.

B: Envy isn't the answer to your problem.

A: I wish you hadn't told me.

B: Why not? As soon as we know that we have done wrong, we should be able to correct it.

A: Of course, if we had known it was wrong, we wouldn't have done it in the first place.

B: Something like that, Allan. But it doesn't always work that way. At times, we know that we're doing wrong, and we still do it.

A: We're only human, Bette. I wish I knew what the future holds for me.

B: Don't be silly, Allan. If you knew what the future was going to look like, life would not be exciting anymore.

A: What's exciting about always being second best?

---

turn around: look (back)
envy: be jealous of
answer: solution
problem: difficulty, unsettled
    question

in the first place: initially
holds: keeps
silly: foolish
exciting: thrilling, wonderful
second best: not the very best

B: Knowing that there is still space for improvement, that's exciting. Isn't it?

A: Gee, you really think deep thoughts, Bette! What a pity I'm already married.

B: Why do you say that? I'm sure Liz would just love it.

A: Because if I were single, I would surely marry a woman like you.

B: You seem so sure that I would marry you, aren't you? If Liz were present, would you repeat what you just said?

A: You're right, Bette. I feel like a heel. One shouldn't wish for things that can't happen. Oh, would that I were wiser!

B: It's never too late to learn, isn't that the truth?

A: I guess I had it coming, didn't I?

B: Don't feel badly, Allan. If you had known how foolish you sounded, you wouldn't have said what you did.

A: Thanks for being so understanding, Bette.

B: Don't mention it. If you hadn't asked for my opinion, I wouldn't have expressed it.

---

improvement: getting better   **had it coming:** expected it
deep: profound, intelligent   **foolish:** silly
heel: terrible person   **opinion:** view, conviction

Narrative: Then, Why Do We Have Wars?

1. Even before recorded time, people killed one another in wars. They were primitive people, and they did not communicate well. Instead of communicating, they threw rocks at each other. Today we have many modern conveniences. We are better able to communicate with one another. But today, people still kill other people in wars. They blow up powerful explosives instead of throwing rocks.

2. If we had lived many thousands of years ago, we would have acted the same way as our ancestors did. Unless we were born as birds or some other kind of nonpredatory animals, we would have killed. So long as people are not willing to remember their past mistakes, they will go on repeating them.

3. Most wars had been fought for "causes." The most frequent excuse or cause for wars in the past was lack of food. If we had inhabited arid land, we would have fought wars to gain fertile land. Then we could grow the food to feed our people. Also, many wars had been waged in the name of God and religious beliefs. Because of religious wars, many people had been hurt and many had died.

---

recorded: set down in writing
primitive: simple
instead of: in place of
conveniences: useful things conducive to comfort
blow up: explode
explosives: something that can explode
acted: done

nonpredatory: not living on other animals
willing: wanting
repeat: do again
cause: reason
lack: want
arid: dry, nonproductive
gain: win
fertile: fruitful

4. If we had wished for people to accept our faith, we would not have killed them. If we had wanted to impress others, we would have impressed them with the kindness of our faith, not its cruelty. Only love and kindness are the real atrributes of a true faith. Such faith puts great value on all life.

5. If I were a leader, I would love all of my people equally. If I had the power to change the world, I would consider the person above all ideals and all causes; I would make this the age of the person. If I had lived thousands of years ago, I would have taught personal dignity and human value. If we had educated the people, knowledge would have liberated them from fear.

6. Nowadays, our leaders promise us many things if they are elected into public office. Everything seems to point toward a better future. We have people of good will; we are better able to communicate with others; people are closer to one another, etc. Then, why do we still have wars? Let's point the way toward the rebirth of faith and confidence in people.

---

wage: carry on

belief: faith

religious: relating to religion

accept: take, receive

impress: affect, have an impact on

cruelty: brutality

attribute: quality

value: worth

equally: alike, the same way, evenly

ideals: goals, principles

age: time

dignity: worth, merit

value: esteem, worth

liberate: free

elect: choose

office: service

point: show, aim

rebirth: born again

confidence: assurance

VOCABULARY

Dialogue Completion

Fill in the missing word in each of the blank spaces of the dialogue.
Select the proper word from the words listed below. One word may be
used more than once. Repeat the sentences aloud.

holds	turn around	hadn't	knew
knew	had	answer	human
envy	should	wrong	as soon as
wouldn't	work	problem	

ALLAN: Every time I _____ _____ , there's someone
who knows more than I. I _____ such people.

BETTE: _____ isn't the _____ to your _____ .

ALLAN: I wish you _____ told me.

BETTE: Why not? _____ we know that we have done wrong,
we _____ be able to correct it.

ALLAN: Of course, if we _____ known it was wrong, we
_____ have done it in the first place.

BETTE: It doesn't always _____ that way, Allan. At times we
know that we're doing _____ , and we still do it.

ALLAN: We're only _____ , Bette. I wish I _____ what
the future _____ for me.

BETTE: Don't be silly, Allan. If you _____ what the future was
going to look like, life _____ be exciting anymore.

Narrative Completion

Fill in each blank space in the text from the list of words and phrases preceding each paragraph. A selection may be used more than once, and more than one word may be used in one blank space. Repeat the sentences aloud.

explosives	communicate	recorded	blow up
primitive	wars	instead	

1. Even before _____ time, people killed one another in
    _____ . They were _____ people, and they did not
    _____ well. _____ of communicating, they threw rocks
    at each other. Today, we are better able to _____ with one
    another. But today, people still kill other people in wars.
    _____ of throwing rocks, they _____ powerful .

repeating	nonpredatory	willing	would
killed	lived	unless	

2. If we had _____ many thousands of years ago, we
    _____ have acted the same way as our ancestors did.
    _____ we were born as birds or some other kind of
    _____ animals, we would have _____ . So long as
    people are not _____ to remember their past mistakes, they
    will go on _____ them.

religious	would	lack	waged
arid	frequent	fertile	had
causes			

3. Most wars had been fought for " _____ ." A frequent cause of
    wars in the past was _____ of food. If we _____ inhab-
    ited _____ land, we _____ have fought wars to gain

land. Many wars _____ been _____ in the name of
God. Many people _____ been hurt and many _____
died because of _____ wars.

cruelty   value   would   had
impress   attributes   accept

4. If we _____ wished for people to _____ our faith,
    we _____ not have killed them. If we _____ wanted to
    _____ others, we _____ have impressed them with the
    kindness of our faith, not its _____ . Only love and kindness
    are the real _____ of a true faith. Such faith puts great
    _____ on all life.

liberate   ideals   equally   value   consider
would   dignity   had   were   age

5. If I a leader, I _____ love all of my people _____ .
    If I the power to change the world, I would _____ the
    person above all _____ and causes; I _____ make this
    the _____ of the person. If I _____ lived thousands
    of years ago, I _____ have taught personal _____ and
    human _____ . If we _____ educated the people,
    knowledge would _____ them from fear.

confidence   communicate   rebirth   elected
point   would   one another

6. Nowadays, our leaders _____ promise us many things if they
    were _____ into public office. Everything seems to
    _____ toward a better future. We have people of good will;
    we are better able to _____ with others; people are closer to
    _____ _____ , etc. Then, why do we still have wars?
    Let's _____ the way toward the _____ of faith and
    _____ in people.

VOCABULARY SUBSTITUTION

Dialogue Completion

Fill in the correct form of the verb in each of the blank spaces of the sentences below. Rewrite and repeat the sentences aloud.

Examples: **(live)**   If we _____ _____ on another planet, we would have acted differently.

If we **had lived** on another planet, we would have acted differently.

(have,   If we _____ _____ the answer to this
know)   problem, we would not have asked the question.

If we **had known** the answer to this problem, we would not have asked the question.

(tell)   If you _____ _____ me, I would never have guessed.

_____

(know)   If we _____ it was wrong, we would not have done it in the first place.

_____

(know)   I wish I _____ what the future holds for me.

_____

(know)   If you _____ what the future was going to look like, life would not be exciting anymore.

_____

(be)   If I _____ single, I would surely marry you.

_____

(be)   If Li _____ present, would you repeat what you said?

_____

(have,   If you _____ _____ how foolish you sounded,
know)   you wouldn't have said what you did.

_____

(have)   If you ___ asked for my opinion, I wouldn't have
expressed it.

_____

Narrative Completion

Fill in the correct form of the verb in each of the blank spaces of the
sentences below. Rewrite and repeat the sentences aloud.

Examples: **(be)**   If I _____ rich, I would be a philanthropist.
If I **were** rich, I would be a philanthropist.

(have,   If I, _____ _____ I wouldn't have
know)   acted silly.

If I **had known,** I wouldn't have acted silly.

(have, live)   If we _____ _____ many thousands of
years ago, we would have acted the same way.

_____

(be)   Unless we _____ born as birds, we would have
killed.

_____

(have)   If we _____ arid land, we would have fought to
gain fertile land.

_____

(have, wish)   If we _____ _____ for people to accept our
faith, we would not have killed them.

_____

(have, want)   If we _____ _____ to impress others,
we would have impressed them with the kindness of
our faith.

_____

(be)   If I _____ a leader, I would love all of my people.

_____

(have)   If I _____ the power to change the world, I
would consider the person above all else.

_____

(have, live)   If I _____ _____ thousands of years ago,
I would have taught personal dignity and human value.

_____

(have, educate)   If we _____ _____ the people, knowledge
would promise us many things.

_____

(be)   If they _____ elected into public office, they
would promise us many things.

_____

PICTOGRAPHS (WORDS IN CONTEXT)

Below are some drawings based on the dialogue presentation. Use the words or phrases listed under each drawing to compose your own dialogue. Words may be used more than once. In addition to those given here, words of your own choosing may be used.

Active vocabulary: turn around, envy, answer, problem, wish, wrong, correct, in the first place, human, future holds

Active vocabulary: deep thoughts, pity I'm married, single, repeat what you said, able to learn, feel bad, foolish, sounded, understanding, don't mention it

Below are some drawings based on the narrative presentation. Use the words or phrases listed below each drawing to compose a short narrative of your own. Words may be used repeatedly. In addition to those listed here, words of your own choosing may be used.

Active vocabulary from paragraphs 1 and 2: recorded time, people killed, one another, wars, primitive, today, modern, communicate, still, throw rocks, blow up, explosives, lived, thousands of years, acted, ancestors, unless, non-predatory animals, so long as, remember past mistakes, repeating

Active vocabulary from paragraphs 3 and 4: fight, causes, frequent, lack of food, arid land, fertile, grow food, many wars, waged, religious belief, people hurt, died, accept faith, kindness, cruelty of faith, attributes, love faith is good, value on all life

Active vocabulary from paragraphs 5 and 6: leader, love all people, power to change, consider, person, above all, ideals, causes, age of person, dignity and human value, educated, knowledge, liberate, fear, nowadays, promote, elected, public office, point toward, future, good will, communicate, wars, rebirth of faith, confidence, people.

Crossword Puzzle

The puzzle below is based on the model narrative presentation. First, fill in the missing words in the sentences, then write them in the puzzle. Read the sentences aloud.

1. Even before _____ time, people killed one another.
   across

2. They were _____ people.
   down

3. If we had _____ thousands of years ago,
   across

4. We _____ have acted the same way.
   across

5. If we had _____ arid land,
   down

6. we would have _____ wars to gain fertile land.
   down

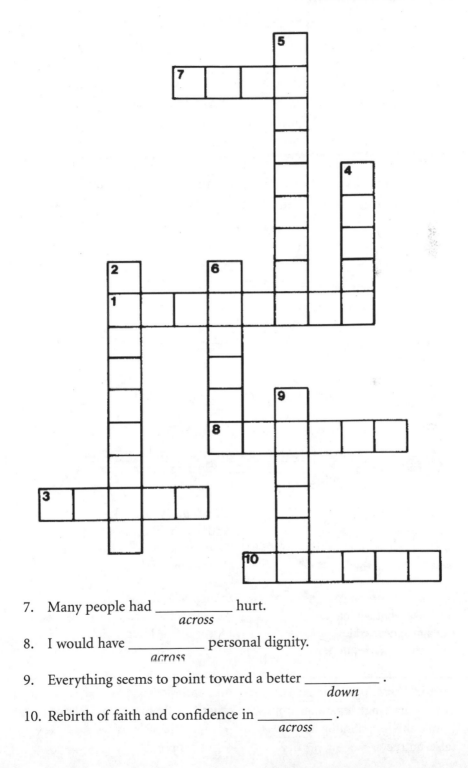

7. Many people had _____ hurt.
   across

8. I would have _____ personal dignity.
   across

9. Everything seems to point toward a better _____ .
   down

10. Rebirth of faith and confidence in _____ .
    across

Song

Below are the words and music of an old folk tune. A folk tune is the same as a *folk song*, which comes to us through the ages, sung generation after generation. No one knows who composed the tune, nor do we know who was the author of its lyrics. We only care about the story told in the old tune. It tells about happiness in love and it speaks about courtship. But it also tells about sadness that comes from untrue love and falsehood. The song sounds a warning to all who are unable to recognize false love.

On Top of Old Smoky

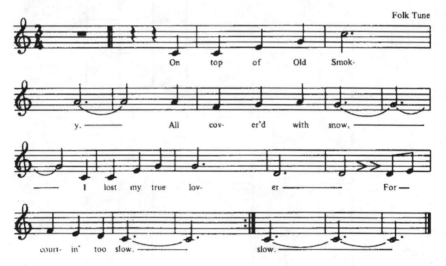

Now courtin's a pleasure
But partin' is grief,
A false hearted lover
Is worse than a thief.

A thief will just rob you
And take what you have,
But a false hearted lover
Will send you to your grave.

They'll hug you and kiss you
And tell you more lies
Than cross-ties on the railroad
Or stars in the skies.

On top of Old Smoky,
All covered with snow,
I lost my true lover
For courtin' too slow.

---

courtin' (courting): trying to enamor
par tin' (parting): separating from one another; splitting up
false: untrue

hug: embrace
cross-ties: beams or posts placed under the rails crosswise for support

GRAMMAR

Explanation and Examples

Whenever we speak about things which are not **really happening,** we use the **past** form of the verb after *if.*

Example: **If** we **lived** in Poland, we would be Polish.

Since we do not live in Poland, we are using the **past** tense of the verb to express a **present unreal** condition (**not true**). We can also say that this sample sentence is an expression **contrary to fact,** which means that it is not true. We will now analyze another contrary-to-fact sentence more thoroughly. This time the happening takes place in the **past.**

Example: **If** we **had known** about the speed trap, **we would** not **have gotten** a speeding ticket.

What are the facts?
1. We did not know about the speed trap.
2. We drove too fast and got a speeding ticket.

Conclusion: **If we had known** about the speed trap,
we **would have driven** slower. (But we didn't, so we got a speeding ticket.)

Did we know about the speed trap? No. That is a condition contrary to fact. But it is not a **present** condition contrary to fact (using the **past** verb form). This is a **past** condition contrary to fact. Here we must use a verb form which goes further back in time than the simple past form of the verb **lived** as used in the first example. This form takes us **behind** the simple past. The form we use is **had known** (second example above) in the use of the verb **to know.** If we used the verb live, we would write the past condition with **had lived.**

We can say that when we refer to a condition that is **contrary to fact,**

unreal or **untrue,** we generally use in the if-clause a tense form which is usually reserved for a different purpose:

1. For **present** contrary-to-fact conditions, we use the **past** verb form: If we **lived** in Poland, we **would be** Polish.
2. For **past** contrary-to-fact conditions, we use the **past perfect** tense (**had + past participle),** when we show that the condition is untrue or contrary to fact: If we **had known** about the speed trap, we **would** not **have gotten** a speeding ticket.

We must remember that in the *I, he, she* and *it* persons, the verb form will not be **was** but **were** when we refer to **present** conditions: **If I were rich.** In the use of **past** conditions, it will follow the pattern of the plural: **If I had been rich.**

Examples: (Present condition)   If **I were** a leader, **I would/could/ should/might** be good to my people.

(Past condition)   If **I had been** a leader, **I would/could/ should/might have been** good to my people.

(Present condition)   If **I were** rich, **I'd** buy a new tie.

(Past condition)   If **I had been** rich, **I would have** bought a new tie.

It is important to learn some additional uses for the conjunction *if* One way to use *if is* to express **condition** as we have done previously.

Examples: **If you have studied** diligently, you **will** pass the exam.
          If you drive carefully, you **won't** get a speeding ticket.

Another use of *if* is to express **contrast;** the meaning often is **although** or **whereas.** It may be used in such sentences as the following:

Examples: **Even if** it rains, we'll go on a picnic.

If you **think** that's bad, wait until you see what happened to me.

If I **was** afraid of traffic before, I am now terrified.

If Sue **is** not a good driver, she is at least a good talker.

Quite frequently, *if* is used in expressing the time element. In the sense of **time,** *if* has the meaning of **when** or **whenever.**

Examples: **If** (or **whenever)** Sue doesn't see the police, she gets a traffic ticket.

If (or **when)** she explains her point to the judge, she won't get a fine.

Whenever *if* is used to express a **degree of difference** between two things, it has the meaning of **just as ... so.**

Examples: **If** what you say is true, it is **just as** bad as what happened to me.

If Sue is unable to convince the judge, she is **still** less able to drive.

If she was disappointed, **so** was the judge.

Practice

Join two sentences into one, expressing an **unreal present condition**.
Read the sentences aloud.

Examples: We don't drive fast. We'd get a speeding ticket if we did.
If we drove fast, we'd get a speeding ticket.
(We'd get a speeding ticket if we drove fast.)

We don't waste time. We'd fail the exam if we did.

If we wasted time, we'd fail the exam.

(We'd fail the exam if we wasted time.)

1. We don't tell a lie. We'd be sorry if we did.

   _____

2. Richard doesn't have a job. He wouldn't be sad if he did.

   _____

3. We smile at people. We wouldn't be happy if we didn't.

   _____

4. Gloria eats well. She wouldn't be pretty if she didn't.

   _____

5. Mark isn't in a hurry. He'd leave early if he were.

   _____

6. Allan doesn't understand life. He'd be happier if he did.

   _____

7. Allan can't get tickets to the show. He'd invite Liz to go out if he did.

   _____

8. We don't visit friends on Sundays. They wouldn't like it if we did.

_____

9. Hiromi doesn't exercise too often. She'd be healthier if she did.

_____

10. We don't go shopping. We'd spend money if we did.

_____

Finish the sentences by selecting the if-clause that describes a **past condition** (contrary to fact). Read the sentences aloud.

Example: Even if Gloria had eaten well,
   a.   she wouldn't be pretty.
   b.   she wouldn't have been pretty.
   Even if Gloria had eaten well, she wouldn't have been pretty.

1. Even if we had told a lie,
   a.   we wouldn't be sorry.
   b.   we wouldn't have been sorry.

_____

2. If Ytaka had studied harder,
   a.   he wouldn't fail the test.
   b.   he wouldn't have failed the test.

_____

3. If we had lived many thousands of years ago,
   a.   we would have acted the same way as our ancestors did.
   b.   we would act the same way as our ancestors did.

_____

4. If we had inhabited arid land,
   a. we would have fought wars to gain fertile land.
   b. we would fight wars to gain fertile land.

   _____

5. They could have grown much food
   a. if they had gained fertile land.
   b. If they gained fertile land.

   _____

6. We would not have killed them
   a. if we had wished for people to accept our faith.
   b. if we wished for people to accept our faith.

   _____

7. If we had wanted to impress others,
   a. we would impress them with our kindness.
   b. we would have impressed them with our kindness.

   _____

8. If I were a leader,
   a. I would love all of my people.
   b. I would have loved all of my people.

   _____

9. If we had educated the people,
   a. knowledge would have liberated them from fear.
   b. knowledge would liberate them from fear.

   _____

10. If we had borrowed money from the bank,
    a. we would have returned it by now.
    b. we would return it by now.

    _____

Write the correct form of the verb to express the **past conditional** (unreal). Read the sentences aloud.

Examples: **(study)** If Joe _____ harder, he wouldn't have failed the course.
If Joe **had studied** harder, he wouldn't have failed the course.

(be able to) If Hiromi _____ remain in Tokyo, she would have done it.
If Hiromi **had been able to** remain in Tokyo, she would have done it.

(talk) If Sofia _____ with her teacher, she would have understood the lesson.

(see) If they _____ the speed trap, they wouldn't have gotten a ticket.

(take) If Mary _____ a vacation, she would have been able to continue to work.

(run away) Mr. Smooth would have married Yalee, if she _____ .

(be able to) If Yalee _____ to marry Mr. Smooth, she would have.

(not be) I would not have believed the story, if I _____ there myself.

(give) If he _____ me the job, I would have accepted it.

(not be)   If my friend _____ late, we would have arrived on time at the concert.

(ask)   If Joe _____ Cindy, she would have told him.

(work)   I wouldn't have finished the job, if I _____ all night.

Identify the uses of if in the following sentences:

Example: If he'd hurry, we'd arrive on time.   _____*conditional*_____

1. Even if I'm sick, I'll go to the ball game.   _____

2. If the baby cries, she gets what she wants.   _____

3. We'll go on a trip, even if I don't feel well.   _____

4. If I disliked Ytaka before, I now hate him.   _____

5. If I am telling you this, it is because I want you to learn.   _____

6. If she was afraid of driving before, she is now terrified.   _____

7. If you have prepared the lesson, you'll impress the teacher.   _____

8. If Hiromi fails the exam, she gets sick.   _____

9. If she talks to her teacher, he will help her.   _____

10. If Akira is unable to understand math in Japanese, he is still less able to understand it in English.   _____

IDEA RECOGNITION

Copy from the model narrative the sentences expressing the following:

1. What had happened before recorded time

    _____

2. What kind of people lived then

    _____

3. How people still kill each other

    _____

4. How we would have acted thousands of years ago

    _____

5. Why we would have killed

    _____

6. For what reason most wars had been fought

    _____

7. Why people wanted fertile land

    _____

8. What happened because of religious wars

    _____

9. How we should impress people

    _____

10. Which are the attributes of a true faith

    _____

11. What you would do as a leader

    _____

12. What kind of age this should be

_____

13. How we could liberate people from fear.

_____

14. What leaders promise nowadays

_____

15. The direction toward which we should point

_____

VOCABULAR Y ENRICHMENT

Substitutions

Change the sentences to express **past unreal condition.** Read the sentences aloud.

Examples: If I were a leader, I would love my people.
            If I had been a leader, I would have loved my people.

            Ytaka and Hiromi would have gotten married if their parents allowed it.
            Ytaka and Hiromi would have gotten married if their parents had allowed it.

1. If we lived many thousands of years ago, we would act the same way as our ancestors did.

_____

_____

2. Unless we were born as some kind of nonpredatory animals, we would kill.

_____

_____

3. If we inhabited arid land, we would fight wars for fertile land.

_____

_____

4. If we wished for people to accept our faith, we would not kill them.

_____

_____

5. We would impress people with kindness if we wanted to impress them.

_____

_____

6. We would tell them if we didn't like them.

_____

_____

7. They could accept our faith if they liked it.

_____

_____

8. If I had the power to change the world, I would consider the person above all ideals and causes.

_____

_____

9. If we educated the people, knowledge would liberate them from fear.

_____

_____

10. We should succeed in coming closer to one another if we are able to communicate.

_____

_____

Lexical Units

Select the word or phrase from the words listed below that best completes each of the sentences. One selection may be used more than once. Read the sentences aloud.

Example: Even before recorded time, people killed each other in wars. They were **primitive** people.

confidence	communicate	rocks
life	grow	repeating
love	blow up	killed
good	ancestors	

1. Primitive people don't communicate with one another. They throw _____ at each other.

2. Today we have modern conveniences. We are better able to _____ with each other.

3. Today people don't throw rocks at each other; they _____ powerful explosives.

4. If we had lived a thousand years ago, we would have acted as our _____ did.

5. So long as people are not willing to remember their past mistakes, they will go on _____ them.

6. If we had fertile land, we could _____ food.

7. If we had wished to impress people, we would not have _____ them.

8. A true faith teaches love and kindness. It puts a great value on all _____ .

9. To be a great leader means to _____ the people.

10. Everything seems to point to a better future because we have people of _____ will.

11. This is the age of a rebirth of faith for the individual. It will bring _____ in people.

Transformations

Restate the sentences in the **past unreal conditional** using **if** and making the sentence negative with *not*. Repeat the sentences aloud.

Examples: I got a speeding ticket because I drove too fast.
If I hadn't driven too fast, I wouldn't have gotten a speeding ticket.

Miguel paid a fine because he didn't see the policeman.
Miguel wouldn't have paid a fine if he had seen the policeman in time.

1. The people always fought because they were not well educated.

_____

_____

2. They weren't able to live in peace because they were primitive.

_____

_____

3. The people threw rocks at each other because they weren't able to communicate.

_____

_____

4. People repeated their mistakes because they weren't willing to remember them.

_____

_____

5. Most wars happened because people needed food.

_____

_____

6. They weren't able to grow food because the land was arid.

_____

_____

7. Many people died because they fought religious wars.

_____

_____

8. We couldn't impress other people because we didn't show them kindness.

_____

_____

For each situation below, make a question beginning with the phrase "What would have happened if . . .?" Then answer the question. Repeat the sentences aloud.

Examples: Abdul drove too fast, so he got a speeding ticket.

Question: What would have happened if Abdul hadn't driven too fast?

Answer: **If Abdul hadn't driven too fast, he wouldn't have gotten a speeding ticket.**

Hiromi came to class late because her alarm clock didn't work.

Question: **What would have happened if the alarm clock had worked?**

Answer: If the alarm clock had worked, Hiromi would have come to class on time.

1.   The people are primitive, so they fight.

Q: _____

A: _____

2.   They cannot communicate, so they throw rocks at each other.

Q: _____

A: _____

3.   Mike was silly, so he laughed at Allan.

Q: _____

A: _____

4. Some people are overweight, so they eat very little.

    Q: _____

    A: _____

5. John helped his friend so he could pass the test.

    Q: _____

    A: _____

6. I was in a hurry, so I forgot the keys.

    Q: _____

    A: _____

7. They didn't review the lessons, so they failed the exam.

    Q: _____

    A: _____

8. Liz wasn't present, so Allan talked badly about her.

    Q: _____

    A: _____

9. Allan felt badly, so he confessed to Bette.

    Q: _____

    A: _____

10. Bette asked Allan's opinion, so he expressed it.

    Q: _____

    A: _____

Special Expressions

Below are some additional conditional structures used in a context
unlike those already discussed. Practice them, then try to compose one
additional sentence for each new structure. Read the sentences aloud.

Examples: **Would** that **I were** rich!
            Would that **we had** permanent peace!

Present meaning
1. If **I were** you, **I wouldn't do** that.

2. If we **weren't** busy, we **would come** to the party.

3. If I still **had** the sailboat, we **would go** sailing.

Past meaning
1. If **I had visited** San Francisco, I **would have rented** a car.

2. If **I'd known** you were coming, **I would have baked** a cake.

3. If people **had been given** a chance, they **might have made** peace
    with each other.

Doubtful conditions
1. **Could** I have this dance?

2. **Would** you mind. . .?

_____

3. **Wouldn't** you and Sue like to join us?

_____

4. If you **would** explain the lesson, I **would** be grateful.

_____

5. If **Henry'd study** more, **he'd get** better grades.

_____

6. **They'd be** doing me a big favor if **they'd** stop the noise.

_____

7. If it **would only stop** raining, we **could have** a picnic.

_____

8. If **only** they **would stop** the noise, we **could get** some sleep.

_____

9. If he **only knew** how much I **love** him!

_____

10. What **would you do** if I **came** to dinner this evening?

_____

11. If **I should happen** to run into Abdul, **I'd be** glad to give him
    your love.

_____

12. If **he ever wished** to come home, **they'd receive** him with open arms.

_____

STEPS IN CREATIVE EXPRESSION

Write the proper form of the verb to complete the sentences below.
Read the sentences aloud.

Example: If we had (**know**) _____**known**_____ it was wrong, we would not
have (**do**) _____**done**_____ it in the first place.

1.   I wish I (**know**) _____ what the future holds for me.

2.   If I (**be**) _____ single, I would surely marry a person like you.

3.   If Liz (**be**) _____ present, would you repeat what you just said?

4.   If you had (**know**) _____ how foolish you sounded, you
wouldn't have (**say**) _____ what you did.

5.   If you hadn't (**ask**) _____ for my opinion, I wouldn't have
(**express**) _____ it.

6.   If we had (**live**) _____ many thousands of years ago, we
would have (**act**) _____ the same way.

7.   If we had (**inhabit**) _____ arid land, we would have (**fight**)
_____ wars to gain fertile land.

8.   If we had (**wish**) _____ for people to accept our faith, we
would not have (**kill**) _____ them.

9.   If we had (**want**) _____ to impress others, we would have
(**impress**) _____ them with the kindness of our faith, not
its cruelty.

10. If I (**be**) _____ a leader, I would love all of my people equally.

Add new words and revise the sentences, if necessary, to suit the
changes in parentheses. Read the sentences aloud.

Example: If we were born in Poland, we would be Polish. (**I**)
If I were born in Poland, I would be Polish.

1.   **I wish you hadn't told me.** (We)

2. As soon as **we** know that **we** did wrong, **we** should be able to correct it. (I)

3. At times **we** know that **we** are doing wrong, and **we** still do it. (she)

4. **I** wish **I** knew what the future holds for me. (he)

5. If **you** knew what the future holds for **you,** life would not be exciting anymore. (we)

6. If **I** were single, **I** would surely marry you. (he)

7. **One** shouldn't wish for things that cannot happen. (we)

8. If **you** had known how foolish **you** sounded, **you** wouldn't have said what **you** did. (she)

9. If **you** hadn't asked for **my** opinion, **I** wouldn't have expressed it. (we, you)

Create a dialogue similar to the model presentation based on the expressions below. (Lolita = L, Hamid = H)

L: Every time _____ there's someone _____ knows.

H: _____ isn't the answer _____ problem.

L: I wish _____ told _____ .

H: As soon as _____ wrong _____ be able _____ correct _____ .

L: If we had known _____ we would _____ first place.

H: Something like that, Lolita. But _____ always

L: _____ only human _____ wish I knew _____ _____ future _____ .

H: _____ silly _____ you knew _____ not exciting _____ .

L: _____ exciting _____ second best?

H: Knowing _____ space for improvement _____ .

Vignette

The Mardi Gras

1. A carnival is a time of having fun: feasting, dressing up in fancy costumes, having parades, listening to music, and generally entertaining friends.

2. The most important carnival in the United States takes place in New Orleans, Louisiana. During the Mardi Gras season, in addition to the parades, many official balls and countless private parties take place.

3. Included in the parades are many floats. They are beautifully designed with a common theme. The floats are really the most important presentation in the parade. In addition, there are many jazz bands and big military orchestras.

---

carnival: festival, exhibition
feasting: eating well
parade: a marching show
entertaining: amusing
season: time

ball: formal dance
countless: too many to count
float: parade exhibit mounted on
　a vehicle
designed: planned

4. Some of the parades take place at night; some are in the daytime. Parades and balls are organized as a way to celebrate Mardi Gras, the New Orleans carnival. At the beginning of each Mardi Gras, a king and queen are chosen. They reign over the carnival as the official royalty. The carnival creates a happy atmosphere.

1. a. What is a carnival?
   b. How do we dress!
   c. What do we eat?
   d. What do we listen to?
   e. Whom do we entertain?

2. a. Where does the most important carnival take place?
   b. In what state is the city of New Orleans?
   c. What is the carnival season called?
   d. What takes place during the carnival?

3. a. What is included in the parades?
   b. How are the floats designed?
   c. What else is included in a parade?

4. a. When do some of the parades take place?
   b. Why are parades and balls organized?
   c. Who is selected at the beginning of Mardi Gras?
   d. What does a carnival create?

5. Do you have a similar celebration in your home town? Describe it.

---

theme: topic   **reign:** rule
band: orchestra   **atmosphere:** feeling, spirit
chosen: selected

COMMENTARY ON MODEL PRESENTATION

Using key words and phrases from the model narrative, comment on the topics presented below.

recorded time	nonpredatory	accept faith
killed one another	animals	impress with kindness
primitive	remember the past	value all alike
communicate	fought for causes	knowledge
threw rocks	lack of food	liberate from fear
modern conveniences	arid land	leaders
wars	fertile land	promise
blow up	feed people	better future
explosives	religious war	people
thousands of years		

1. a. Tell what has always happened.
   b. Discuss the difference between primitive and modern wars.
   c. Describe the causes of wars.
   d. Comment on how we can stop wars.
   e. Tell what we must point to.

2. a. Discuss the points in the model narrative that you like.
   b. Discuss the points in the model narrative that you don't like.
   c. Give an appropriate title to your composition.

FREE COMPOSITION

Dialogue Improvisation

Compose your own dialogue, using the situation given below.

1. Your friend says that she is envious of people who know more.

2. You tell her not to worry—she can learn more.

3. She says that she has been trying to learn, but is unable to.

4. You tell her that she is progressing because she knows what she wants.

5. She tells you that you are a good friend.

6. You assure her that this is what friends are for.

7. She says that she'd like to look into her future.

8. You tell her that life would not be exciting if she could see the future.

9. She says that it was silly to wish the impossible.

Fill in the Missing Dialogue

For each of the drawings below, write your own dialogue which describes the action.

Compose a short narrative, building on the expressions given below.

1. . . . before recorded time . . . primitive people . . . communicate well. . . better able . . . each other. . . they don't throw . . . blow up . . . . explosives. . .

2. . . . had lived . . . thousand years. . . have acted . . . ancestors. . . unless . . . born as birds . . . would have. . . . so long as . . . willing to remember. . . past mistakes. . . repeating. . .

3. . . . wars had been fought. . . frequent excuse . . . lack of food . . . if we had . . . arid land . . . to gain . . . grow food . . . many people . . . hurt . . . died.

4. . . . wished for people . . . accept. . . would not. . . killed them . . . if we . . . wanted . . . impress . . . kindness of our faith . . . cruelty. . . real attributes. . . great value . . . life.

CHAPTER NINE

Our Dream House

Keeping Up With the Joneses

	Present Continuous	Future		Future Perfect
	am	*will be*	*past + participle*	*will have been*
	being			
	is +	*am*		*+*
	past			
	are participle			*past participle*
		is going to be	*past + participle*	
		are going to be		

MODEL PRESENTATION

Dialogue: Our Dream House

(Pam = P, Maggie = M)

P: You know, every American family hopes that some day they can build their "dream house."

M: I guess it's true. We had to wait many years until ours was finally completed.

P: Ours is still being worked on.

M: Why does it take this long?

P: There are many reasons. First, the old plans have been changed by the architects. Then, the building materials were't delivered on time. After that delay, a carpenters" strike was organized. I'm not sure what kept us going. We almost gave up on the house altogether.

M: I can understand how you feel, Pam. But I'll bct you'll enjoy it after all of the trouble you're going through to have it completed.

P: Especially the children; they'll have the extra rooms. Also, the younger two will be taken to school on a school bus, so they'll meet new friends each day.

M: Plus, I've heard that children are being treated in a special way at rural schools. Hot lunches are being served daily. Milk is donated by the county government at lunch time.

P: We won't have to envy the country folks any more.

---

dream house: ideal home
completed: finished
plans: designs
delivered: brought
delay: slowdown
strike: protest

organized: instituted
treated: cared for
rural: country
donated: given
envy: begrudge
folks: people

M: Our old house was put up for sale. I'm sure it will be sold soon.

P: I wish you luck. You know, our present home isn't over fifteen years old and it's being renovated already. Anyway, our oldest daughter Vicky is going off to college next month.

M: I had no idea you had a college-age daughter. Too bad she won't be able to enjoy the new house.

P: As they say, time marches on. She's been invited to stay with some friends of ours, and she's thrilled.

M: She'll be missed at home, won't she?

P: Yes, we're a closely knit family.

M: So are we. I'd miss my children if they were to leave home.

P: I'm sure you would.

M: Well, whatever happens, we must make the best of it.

P: Spoken like a true philosopher.

M: Besides, Vicky's semester will be finished in no time at all. Then she can come visiting.

P: We're certainly looking forward to that. I have to run along now. Say hello at home.

M: You, too.

P: So long.

---

put up: offered
renovated: renewed, remodeled
thrilled: excited

closely knit: intimate
miss: feel the absence of
make the best of: try to succeed

Narrative: Keeping Up With the Joneses

1. "Keeping up" is a popular pastime for most American families. It generally means that people keep an eye on their neighbors. They do this because they wish to know when a new car will be bought, what kind of a car it is, etc.

2. If your neighbor buys an expensive T.V. set, you'll want to know where it was bought and how much it cost. When you find out these facts, you'll go out and buy a T.V. set which can be compared favorably with that of your neighbor's.

3. People are often being talked about, and they learn to gossip about others. That is also a kind of a game that is being played quite often. When you're away from your weekly social gathering you will be talked about. Oftentimes, you are not being talked about with kindness. That should not be the cause for worry.

4. This "keeping up with the Joneses" is an example of the competitive spirit of the American people. As it happens, most people believe that material possessions are regarded as "status symbols." Great

---

pastime: recreation
keep an eye: spy
buy: purchase
facts: things
compare: liken
favorably: advantageously
often: frequently
gossip: talk in a chatty way about others
game: entertainment

social: friendly; relating to the interaction of human beings
gathering: party
cause: reason
worry: distress
competitive: based on rivalry
regarded: thought of, considered
material: physical
possessions: belongings
status symbols: things that suggest wealth

wealth and the earning power of a person are displayed in the clothes that are worn, the car that is driven, and the places that are frequented.

5. No longer does one control one's life style; on the contrary, a person's thoughts and habits are being dictated by the life style. In conclusion, we might add that society is being weakened by its increasing search for self-gratification. People would be better served if they chose to become stronger spiritually. Happiness is in the mind, not in the bankroll.

VOCABULARY

Dialogue Completion

Retell the model dialogue by filling in the missing word. Select the proper word from the words listed below. One word may be used more than once. Repeat the dialogue aloud for correct pronunciation.

love	put	organized	take
like	decided	delivered	being
renovated	moving	completed	
taken	been	looking	

DAVID: My house was finally _____ .

SARA: Ours is still _____ worked on.

DAVID: Why does it _____ this long?

---

wealth: riches, affluence
earning: money-making
displayed: shown
frequent: visit
control: dominate
dictated: forced

weakened: softened
increasing: rising
self-gratification: self-satisfaction
chose: selected
bankroll: fortune, supply
  of money

SARA: The plans have _____ changed suddenly.

DAVID: Were the materials _____ on time?

SARA: Yes, but unfortunately a carpenters' strike was _____ at the same time.

DAVID: I'll bet you'll enjoy it when it's _____ .

SARA: I know that the children will. They'll be _____ to school on a school bus.

DAVID: I didn't know you were _____ that far out of the city.

SARA: Yes, we _____ to try country living. Our old property was up for sale.

DAVID: Hey, that's funny. I've been _____ for a house. Is it being _____ ?

SARA: Yes it is. If you'd _____ , I'll show it to you tomorrow.

DAVID: I'd _____ it. At what time?

SARA: Is 10:00 a.m. okay?

DAVID: See you at ten.

SARA: Bye, now.

Narrative Completion

Fill in each blank space in the text from the list of words and phrases preceding each paragraph. A selection may be used more than once, and more than one word may be used in one blank space. Repeat the sentences aloud.

"keeping up"   keep an eye   buys   pastime

1. _____ is a popular _____ for most American families. It means that people _____ on their neighbor. They do this because they wish to know when their neighbor _____ something new.

compare   cost   neighbor

2. If your _____ buys an expensive T.V. set, you'll want to know
    how much it _____ . You'll want your own T.V. to
    _____ favorably to that of your neighbor's.

talked   game   played   being

3. People are often _____ talked about. That is a kind of a
    _____ that is _____ by many people. At social gather-
    ings, you'll be _____ about. Oftentimes, you are not
    _____ about with kindness.

frequented	example	material	symbols
driven	competitive	is	believe
displayed	worn		

4. This "keeping up with the Joneses" is an _____ of the
    _____ spirit of the American people. Most people
    _____ that _____ possessions are regarded as "status
    _____ ." Wealth is _____ in the clothes that are
    _____ , the car that _____ _____ , and the
    places that are _____ .

VOCABULARY SUBSTITUTION

Dialogue Completion

Fill in the missing word in each of the blank spaces of the dialogue.
Select the proper word or phrase from the words listed below. The same
expression may be used more than once. Read the sentences aloud.

enjoy	finished	changed	instituted
worked	brought	protest	designs
slowdown	long	ideal home	

ARTHUR: Every American family wants an _____ _____ .

SARA: We waited many years before ours was _____

_____ .

ARTHUR: Ours is still being _____ on.

SARA: Why does it take this _____ ?

ARTHUR: The old _____ have been _____ by the architects.

SARA: Why?

ARTHUR: Because the building materials weren't _____ on time.

SARA: That must have been quite a _____ .

ARTHUR: Yes, and right after that, a carpenter's _____ was

_____ .

SARA: I'll bet you'll _____ the house after all the trouble
you've gone through to have it _____ .

ARTHUR: You're so right.

Narrative Completion

Fill in the missing word in each of the blank spaces of the narrative.
Select the proper word or phrase from the words listed preceding each
paragraph below. Read the sentences aloud.

spy   recreation

1. "Keeping up with the Joneses" is a popular _____ for most
   Americans. It generally means that people _____ on their
   neighbors.

advantageously   liken   purchase(d)   things

2. If your neighbor buys an expensive T.V. set, you'll want to know
   where it was _____ and how much it cost. When you find
   out these _____ , you'll go out and _____ a T.V. set
   which will _____ _____ to that of your neighbor's.

entertainment	distress	reason	frequently
talk in a chatty way	party	kindness	

3. People are _____ talked about, and they learn to _____ about others. That is also a kind of _____ that is being played quite _____ . When you're away from your weekly _____ , you will be talked about. Oftentimes, you are not being talked about with _____ . That should not be a _____ for _____ .

practical	visited	money-making	seen
worn	driven	belongings	shown
riches	based on rivalry		

4. This "keeping up with the Joneses" is an example of the _____ spirit of the American people. As it happens, most people believe that _____ are being _____ as "status symbols." Great _____ and the _____ power of a person are being _____ in the clothes that are _____ , the car that is _____ , and the places which will be _____ .

rising	selected	satisfaction	dominate
forced	softened	fortune	

5. No longer does one _____ one's life style; on the contrary, a person's thoughts and habits are being _____ by the life style. In conclusion, we might add that society is being _____ by its _____ search for self-_____ . People would be better served if they _____ to become stronger spiritually instead of chasing after a _____ .

PICTOGRAPHS (WORDS IN CONTEXT)

Below are some drawings based on the dialogue presentation. Use the words or phrases listed under each drawing to compose your own dialogue. Words may be used more than once. In addition to those given here, words of your own choosing may be used. Read the sentences aloud.

Active vocabulary: dream house, wait, years, completed, enjoy, the children, rural, treated, envy, country folks, renovated, old home sold, wish you luck

Active vocabulary: worked on, plans changed, strike, organized, kept us going, gave up, enjoy after the trouble, completed

Below are some drawings based on the narrative presentation. Use the words or phrases listed below each drawing to construct a short narrative of your own. Words may be used repeatedly. In addition to those listed here, words of your own choosing may be used.

Active vocabulary from paragraphs 1 and 2: keeping up, pastime, keep an eye on neighbors, new T.V., new car, expensive, how much it costs, facts, compare favorably, showroom

Active vocabulary from paragraphs 3, 4, and 5: often, gossip, social gathering, competitive spirit, material possessions, regarded, status s ymbol, earning power, displayed, clothes, cars, places frequented, control life style, thoughts and habits, dictated, society weakened, increasing search, self-gratification, better served, spiritually stronger, happiness

Crossword Puzzle

The puzzle below is based on the model dialogue presentation. First, fill in the missing words in the sentences, then write them in the puzzle.

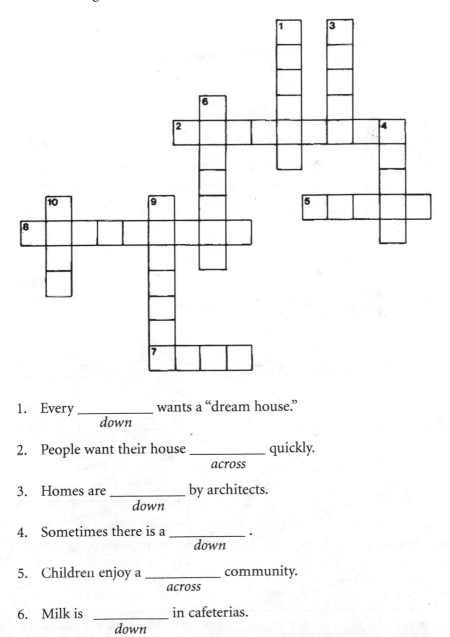

1. Every _____ wants a "dream house."
   down

2. People want their house _____ quickly.
   across

3. Homes are _____ by architects.
   down

4. Sometimes there is a _____ .
   down

5. Children enjoy a _____ community.
   across

6. Milk is _____ in cafeterias.
   down

7. The old house will be _____ soon.
   across

8. Some old homes are being _____ .
   across

9. Time _____ on.
   down

10. One must make the _____ of it.
    down

Song

This folk song, which is also a puzzle, is called *The Riddle Song*. **Riddle** means that there are questions to be solved. The questions are being asked in the second stanza and answered in the third stanza. Read the song before you sing it in class and try to guess the answers before you see them in the third stanza.

The Riddle Song
(I Gave My Love A Cherry)

Folk Tune

I gave my love a cher-ry that has no stone; I
gave my love a chick-en that has no bone; I
gave my love a ring —— that has no end; I
gave my love a ba-by with no cry-in'. ——

How can there be a cherry without a stone?	A cherry when it's bloomin', it has no stone;
How can there be a chicken without a bone?	A chicken when it's pippin', it has no bone;
How can there be a ring that has no end?	A ring when it's rollin', it has no end;
How can there be a baby with no cryin'?	A baby when it's sleepin', there's no cryin'.

cryin': crying	**pipping:** making high-pitched noises
blooming: blossoming	**rolling:** turning over and over

(Note: The apostrophe after the words *bloomin', pippin', rollin', and sleepin'* signifies the missing letter g in colloquial English.)

Now, answer the following questions:

1. What is a cherry when it is in bloom?
2. What is a pipping chicken?
3. Can you roll a ring?
4. Why doesn't a baby cry when it's sleeping?

GRAMMAR

Explanation and Examples

There are three points to remember in the transformation of a sentence from the **active** to the **passive** voice:

1. The **object** of the transitive verb (active voice) becomes the **subject** of the sentence in the passive voice.

2. The verb is replaced by the corresponding form of the verb **be** plus the **past participle** of the main verb.

3. The original subject of the sentence may be used after the verb (as **indirect object**), preceded by the preposition **by.**

Examples: **Ahmed kicked the ball.**   (active)
               subj.   verb   object

                      The ball was kicked by Ahmed.   (passive)
                          subj.   verb ind. object

                      Sue drove the car.   (active)
                      subj. verb   object

                      The car was driven by Sue.   (passive)
                       subj.   verb ind. object

DIAGRAM

ACTIVE: Sue   drove   the car.

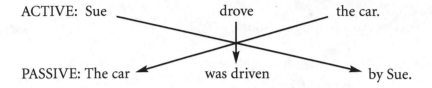

PASSIVE: The car   was driven   by Sue.

Other transformations may be applied to the following:

1. The objects of nonseparable two-word verbs

2. The objects of separable two-word verbs.

Examples: Ahmed **cared for** his wife (he cared for her), (active)
            His wife was cared for by Ahmed, (passive)

                Henry **called up** his parents (he called them up), (active)
            His parents were called up by Henry, (passive)

The main function of the **passive** voice in English is to convey action without naming the one who acts:

Examples: 1. English is spoken here.
             2. Homework is done on time.
             3. Invitations have been sent out.

The above three sentences may also be expressed in the active voice without naming specific actors:

Examples: 1. They speak English here.
             2. They do homework on time.
             3. They have sent out the invitations.

As a summary, it would be proper to remember that **voice** in English grammar refers to the **active** or **passive** use of the verb. In the **active voice,** the *doer* of the action is the grammatical **subject** and the *receiver* of the action is the grammatical **object.** What we have changed, in transforming the active sentence into a passive sentence, is that the original *receiver* of the action is now the grammatical **subject** and the original *doer* of the action is the grammatical **object** of the preposition **by.** The same action is expressed **indirectly.**

Example: The dog (*doer of the action*) bit my uncle (*receiver of the action*), (active)

My uncle (*receiver of the action*) was bitten by the dog (*doer of the action*), (passive)

Practice

Transform the following sentences into the passive voice. Remember to use the same tense in the passive as it was in the active sentence. Read the sentences aloud.

Example: Pablo found the money. (active)
            The money was found by Pablo. (passive)

1. Martha bought a dress.

    _____

2. Carl drives the car.

    _____

3. The thief stole my wallet.

    _____

4. The police caught the thief.

    _____

5. Sue has written a good composition.

   _____

6. Akira examined the suits.

   _____

7. The carpenters finished my room.

   _____

8. She is selling her house.

   _____

9. The government donates milk.

   _____

10. The bus takes the children to school.

   _____

Insert the indicated tense of the passive in the blanks below. Read the sentences aloud.

Example: I'm sure the car _____ somewhere. (**find**-future)
           I'm sure the car **will be found** somewhere.

1. Don't you think the house _____ soon? (**finish**-future)

2. The trip _____ because of rain. (**cancel**-past)

3. Many performances _____ on Sundays. (**give**—present)

4. Contact lenses _____ by many. (**wear**—future)

5. Much money _____ to charity. (**donate**—pres. perf.)

6. Friends _____ not often _____ . (**neglect**—present)

7. The book _____ by the author. (**sign**—future)

8. Many animals _____ by human wars. (**kill**—pres. perf.)

9. Documents _____ usually _____ by officials. (**signed**-present)

10. The football _____ very far. (**kick**-past)

11. The mail _____ by the mail person. (**pick up**-past cont.)

12. Letters _____ to the house. (**deliver**-pres. perf.)

13. The exam _____ to all students. (**give**-future)

14. Many cars _____ by my mechanic. (**fix**-pres. perf.)

15. Paco _____ by Laura. (**kiss**-past)

IDEA RECOGNITION

Copy from the model narrative the sentences expressing the following:

1. The idea of a popular pastime for most Americans

   _____

2. Whom the Americans keep an eye on

   _____

3. Why they keep an eye on their neighbor

   _____

4. What people do when they find out that their neighbor bought some thing new

   _____

5. What your T.V. set should compare to

   _____

6. What people often do at social gatherings

   _____

7. What most people believe about material possessions

_____

8. Ideas about "status symbols"

_____

9. What controls a person's thoughts

_____

10. How society is weakened

_____

VOCABULAR Y ENRICHMENT

Paraphrasing

The following are paraphrases of expressions or words from the model narrative. Find those expressions and write them on the blank lines below. Repeat the sentences aloud.

Example: They were planning to build a house.
            They intended to build a house.

1. a. People spy on one another

    _____

    _____

    b. They want to be informed

    _____

    _____

2. a. Know how expensive the T.V. set is

   _____

   _____

   b. You'll want to buy as expensive a set as your neighbor

   _____

   _____

3. a. People tell about each other

   _____

   _____

   b. In your absence, they talk about you

   _____

   _____

   c. Don't be alarmed about it

   _____

   _____

4. a. This is not part of rivalry

   _____

   _____

   b. People consider belongings as important

   _____

   _____

    c.   What you have shows how you are

_____

_____

    d.   Where you go tells about you

_____

_____

5. a.   People depend on living standards

_____

_____

    b.   Wanting things for oneself makes one weaker

_____

_____

    c.   Mental attitudes are most important

_____

_____

Lexical Units

Select the word or phrase from the words listed below that best completes each of the sentences. One selection may be used more than once. Read the sentences aloud.

Example: People **keep an eye** on one another.
                They **want to know** about each other.

better	compare	material	spiritual
kind	buy	controlled	wish to know
talked	status symbol		

1. They keep an eye on their neighbors. They do this because they

    _____ when the neighbors buy things.

2. When they find out the facts, they'll go out and _____ the same things as their neighbors did.

3. You must know how much your neighbor's T.V. set costs. Only then will yours _____ favorably.

4. When you're away from a party, don't be surprised if you're _____ about.

5. Talking about people is called "gossip." This type of talk is not always _____ .

6. Many people wish to impress others. They do this with _____ possessions.

7. People buy things because they think it will make them appear _____ .

8. What you buy and where you frequent seems important. It is all regarded as a _____ .

9. Not many persons can control their life style. When this happens, they're being _____ by the life style.

10. Desire for material things weakens society. Happiness comes as a result of _____ strength.

STEPS IN CREATIVE EXPRESSION

Answer the questions using the **passive** voice. Read the sentences aloud.

Example: What did we have to wait for? (the house—complete)
           We had to wait until the house was completed.

1. What is being done now? (our house—work on)

   _____

2. What happened to delay the work? (materials—deliver)

   _____

3. When will they complete the work? (next week)

   _____

4. How will the children go to school? (bus—pick up)

   _____

5. What does the government donate at lunch time? (milk)

   _____

6. What happened to the old house? (put up—sale)

   _____

7. How is the old house? (renovate)

   _____

8. Who'll miss Vicky? (at home)

   _____

9. What will Vicky spend money on? (new dress)

   _____

Underline the **passive** voice first. Write the **tense** of the passive voice on the line. Read the sentences aloud.

Example: The car **was hit** by a train.   _____*past*_____

1. The house was finally completed.   _____

2. Work is being done.   _____

3. Plans have been changed.   _____

4. Materials weren't delivered.   _____

5. A strike was organized.   _____

6. They'll be taken to school.   _____

7. They're being treated well.   _____

8. Lunch is being served daily.   _____

9. Milk has been donated by the county.   _____

10. The old house was being renovated.   _____

Create a dialogue similar to the model presentation.
(Ron = R, Patricia = P)

R: My house _____ worked on.

P: _____ so long?

R: Workers _____ strike _____ organized.

P: _____ getting tired _____ .

R: _____ kept us going.

P: _____ enjoy when _____ completed.

R: Our children _____ taken to school _____ .

P: That's nice _____ at rural schools.

R: Yes _____ country folks _____ .

P: _____ luck.

R: Thanks.

P: See _____ later.

R: So long.

Vignette

Auto Racing: The Magic of Indy

1. Each year on Memorial Day, people come from all over the world to experience one of the great auto races: the Indianapolis 500. It is called this because the race goes a distance of five hundred miles.

2. This is the oldest auto race and probably the most dangerous one. There have been sixty-five deaths caused by the Indy track. Some people who come are attracted by the excitement of racing; others are coaxed by the fascination of danger and death.

3. Soon after the Indianapolis 500 auto race was inaugurated in 1911, other auto races were introduced elsewhere. There is a big event in

---

magic: charm
Memorial Day: U.S. legal
  holiday commemorating
  dead servicemen
race: contest, competition
distance: course

attracted: captivated
coaxed: persuaded
inaugurated: started
elsewhere: somewhere else
event: happening
winding: curvy

Sebring, Florida. It is much shorter than the Indy 500, although quite as dangerous a contest over a winding 5.2 mile course. However, the longest auto road race is the LeMans. People enjoy the excitement of auto racing in America.

Discuss the following questions:

1. Do you like auto racing?
2. Does auto racing excite people? Why? Why not?
3. Is there an auto race in your country?
4. Would you participate in an auto race? Why? Why not?

COMMENTARY ON MODEL PRESENTATION

Give a summary of the model narrative presentation based on the outline below.

1. a. What does "keeping up" mean?
   b. Why do people keep up?
   c. Whom do people keep up with?

2. a. What will you want to know?
   b. Why will you want to know it?
   c. What will you do when you find out?

3. a. What do we call this game?
   b. When do people talk about others?
   c. Where do they talk about others?
   d. In what manner do people talk about others?

4. a. Why is "keeping up" competitive?
   b. What do most people believe?
   c. What does a person display?
   d. How is a person judged by others?

5. a. How is a person controlled?
   b. By what are a person's thoughts and habits dictated?
   c. How is society weakened?
   d. What can strengthen society?
   e. What is happiness?

6. a. Discuss the points in the model narrative that impressed you the most.
   b. Discuss the points in the model narrative that impressed you the least.
   c. Tell what you have learned from the model narrative.
   d. Give an appropriate title to your composition.

FREE COMPOSITION

Dialogue Improvisation

Compose your own dialogue using the paraphrases below. Read the sentences aloud.

1. You ask your friend what he'd like best.
2. Your friend responds that he'd love to have a big house built.
3. You tell your friend that it would take a long time to have it built.
4. He says that it is worth waiting for.
5. You ask him where he'd like to live.
6. He says he'd prefer to live in the country.
7. You are not sure why.
8. Your friend explains about good rural schools and how children are being treated.
9. You say that you'll have your old house sold.
10. Your friend tells you to have the old house renovated.
11. You think that's a good idea.
12. You say your good-byes.

Fill in the Missing Dialogue

For each of the drawings below, write your own dialogue which describes the action.

Compose a short narrative, building on the expressions given below.
Read the narrative aloud.

1. . . . popular pastime . . . keep an eye on . . . wish to know. . .

2. if your neighbor buys . . . how much it cost. . . . find out these facts. . .
   compare favorably. . .

3. people are . . . talked about . . . gossip about others   game that is
   played. . . . When you're away . . . social gathering . . . talked about. . .

4. . . . not competitive spirit . . . as it happens, most people believe that
   material possessions. . . great wealth and the earning power. . .
   displayed in clothes . . . and places. . .

5. no longer . . . control. . . on the contrary . . . thoughts . . . dictated by
   the life style. . . we might add that society . . . increasing search . . .
   people would be better served . . . become stronger. . .

CHAPTER TEN

Let's Continue

The Genius of Invention

IN THIS CHAPTER

Words to Remember

Direct Statement or Direct Quote

Reported Speech or Indirect Statement

Quotation Mark (" ") and Colon (:)

Wh- *questions = why, where, what, when, who, how*

MODEL PRESENTATION

Dialogue: Let's Continue

(David = D, Molly = M)

D: Why does everyone tell me "You must go on! You have to continue!"

M: Maybe because they know that you start too many things, but you finish few.

D: That's not true.

M: What do you mean?

D: Well, when I start something, I'll finish it, if I'm interested.

M: But if you lose interest?

D: Then I'll give it up.

M: That's exactly why people tell you to continue. You've lost interest in too many things.

D: Come to think of it, they may be right.

M: What are you going to do about it?

D: I'll try to improve myself.

M: The best way to improve ourselves is to admit our faults.

D: That's the most difficult task of all.

M: True. But it's also a sign of great personal courage.

D: Why do you say that?

---

go on: continue
start: begin
finish: accomplish
interested: curious
give up: stop
exactly: precisely
do about (it): correct (it)

improve: better
admit: acknowledge
fault: weakness
personal: individual
courage: valor
honest: true

M: Because to admit one's faults means to be honest with oneself.

D: And that is very difficult?

M: Yes, it is. That's why a great man once said, "To your own self be true. . . ."

D: I know, I know, ". . . and the truth shall make you free."

M: I hope you'll remember this. . .

D: . . . and I'll continue.

Narrative: The Genius of Invention

1. It is almost unbelievable when we think that more scientific and technological progress was made in the last decade than in all of the past few centuries of our civilization. Of course, this seems to be true especially when we regard this issue from the point of view of available everyday household conveniences.

2. What we must always remember is the fact that all present and future developments are only possible because of the work which was done in the past. Everything we do or think goes back to something or to someone in the past. Progress is a result of cumulative knowledge. In fact, someone once said, "There is nothing new under the sun."

3. If we ponder the above statement carefully, we may conclude the following: (1) someone started the task before us but was unable to finish it; (2) others continued and progressed to the point of their maximum ability; (3) the foundation they had laid made it possible for us to go a small distance further; and (4) others will come and improve our conditions in the future.

---

unbelievable: unthinkable
progress: improvement
decade: ten years
century: one hundred years
regard: look at
issue: matter

conveniences: comforts, useful things conducive to comfort
development: advancement
ponder: consider, think deeply
carefully: cautiously
maximum: best, greatest, highest

4. Thus, we pick up where our predecessors left off and continue from there. All human development owes a debt of gratitude to the past. Continuity is present in all endeavors if it is to be lasting and not momentary. And in all of our endeavors, we can repeat quite honestly the old adage "Necessity is the mother of invention."

VOCABULARY

Dialogue Completion

Fill in the missing word in each of the blank spaces of the dialogue. Select the proper word from the words listed below. One word may be used more than once. Repeat the sentences aloud for correct pronunciation.

courage	improve	interested	possible	do about
mean	faults	give up	true	admit
interest	finish	start	go on	

DAVID: Why do people tell me "You must _____ ."

MOLLY: You _____ too many things, but you _____ few.

DAVID: That's not _____ .

MOLLY: What do you _____ ?

DAVID: I finish things if I'm _____ .

MOLLY: And if you lose _____ ?

---

foundation: base
distance: extent
pick up: start
predecessors: ancestors
left off: stopped
development: growth
gratitude: thanks

continuity: uninterrupted succession, uniformity
lasting: enduring
momentary: temporary
endeavor: work
adage: proverb, saying

DAVID: Then I _____ _____ .

MOLLY: What are you going to _____ _____ it?

DAVID: I'll try to _____ myself.

MOLLY: First, you should _____ your _____ .

DAVID: I can't promise.

MOLLY: That's difficult, but it's _____ . It's a sign of great

_____

DAVID: Well, if you think it's important, I'll start to _____
myself.

MOLLY: I'm glad you're not going to _____ _____
this time.

DAVID: This time, I'll _____ .

Narrative Completion

Fill in each blank space in the text from the list of words and phrases
preceding each paragraph. A selection may be used more than once,
and more than one word may be used in one blank space.

regard	conveniences	decade	progress
issue	unbelievable	centuries	

1. It is almost _____ when we think that more scientific and
    technological _____ was made in the last _____ than
    in all of the past few _____ of our civilization. Of course,
    this seems to be true especially when we _____ this
    _____ from the point of view of available everyday
    household _____ .

cumulative	developments	sun	progress
remember	new	past	work

2. What we must always _____ is the fact that all present and
    future _____ are only possible because of the _____
    which was done in the _____ . Everything we do or think
    goes back to something or to someone in the _____ .
    _____ is a result of _____ knowledge. In fact, someone
    once said, "There is nothing _____ under the _____ ."

finish	improve	ponder
progressed	foundation	carefully
maximum	task	distance

3. If we _____ the above statement _____ , we may
    conclude the following: (1) someone started the _____
    before us but was unable to _____ it; (2) others continued
    and _____ to the point of their _____ ability; (3) the
    _____ they had laid made it possible for us to go a small
    _____ further; (4) others will come and _____
    on our work in the future.

invention	lasting	continuity	endeavors
development	adage	predecessors	

4. Thus, we pick up where our _____ left off and
    continue from there. All human _____ owes a debt of
    gratitude to the past. _____ is present in all _____
    if it is to be _____ . And in all of our _____ , we can
    repeat quite honestly the old _____ "Necessity is the mother
    of _____ ."

VOCABULAR Y SUBSTITUTION

Dialogue Completion

Fill in the missing word in each of the blank spaces of the dialogue.
Select the proper word or phrase from the words listed below.
Read the sentences aloud.

correct	stop	curious	continue	curiosity
so	ant	accomplish	better	begin

DAVID: Why do people tell me? "You must _____ ."

MOLLY: You _____ too many things but you _____ few.

DAVID: That's not true .

MOLLY: What do you mean to say?

DAVID: I accomplish things, if I'm _____ .

MOLLY: And if you lose your _____ ?

DAVID: Then I _____ .

MOLLY: How are you going to _____ it?

DAVID: I'll try to _____ myself.

Narrative Completion

Fill in the missing word in each of the blank spaces of the narrative.
Select the proper word or phrase from the words listed preceding
each paragraph below. Read the sentences aloud.

matter	look at	three hundred years	comforts
unthinkable	improvement	ten years	common

1. It is almost _____ when we realize that more scientific and technological _____ was made in the last _____ than in the past _____ of our civilization. Of course, this seems to be true especially when we _____ it from the point of view of available _____ household _____ .

before us	take into consideration	background
advancements	improvement	job
novel	collective	

2. What we must always _____ is the fact that all present and future _____ are only possible because of the _____ done _____ . Everything we do or think goes back to something or to someone in our _____ . _____ is a result of knowledge. In fact, someone once said, "There is nothing _____ under the sun."

extent	best	cautiously	better	improved
job	base	consider	accomplish	

3. If we _____ the above statement _____ , we may conclude the following: (1) someone started the _____ before us but was unable to _____ it; (2) others continued and _____ on it to the point of their _____ ability; (3) the _____ they had laid made it possible for us to go a small _____ further; and (4) others will come and _____ our work in the future.

enduring	uniformity	proverb	growth	discovery
stopped	ancestors	work	start	thanks

4. Thus we _____ where our _____ had _____ and continue from there. All human _____ owes a debt of _____ to the past. _____ is present in all _____ if it is to be _____ . And in all of our _____ , we can repeat quite honestly the old _____ "Necessity is the mother of _____ .

PICTOGRAPHS (WORDS IN CONTEXT)

Below are some drawings based on the dialogue presentation. Use the words or phrases listed under each drawing to compose your own dialogue. The same words may be used more than once. In addition to those given here, words of your own choosing may be used. Repeat the sentences aloud.

Active vocabulary: go on, continue, start, finish, true, what do you mean, interest, do about, improve

Active vocabulary: improve ourselves, admit faults, sign of personal courage, honest, difficult, be true

Below are some drawings based on the narrative presentation. Use the words or phrases listed below each drawing to construct a short narrative of your own. Words may be used repeatedly. In addition to those listed here, words of your own choosing may be used. Repeat the sentences aloud.

Active vocabulary from paragraphs 1 and 2: unbelievable, scientific, technological, progress, last decade, past centuries, civilization, regard this issue, everyday conveniences, developments, done in the past, goes back, progress, result, cumulative knowledge, nothing new

Active vocabulary from paragraphs 3 and 4: ponder, statement, carefully, concluded, someone started, unable, finish, continued, point of ability, foundation laid, possible for us, small distance further, improve, conditions, pick up, predecessors, human development, debt of gratitude, continuity, endeavor, lasting, not momentary, necessity, mother, invention

Crossword Puzzle

The puzzle below is based on the model narrative presentation. First, fill in the missing words in the sentences, then write them in the puzzle.

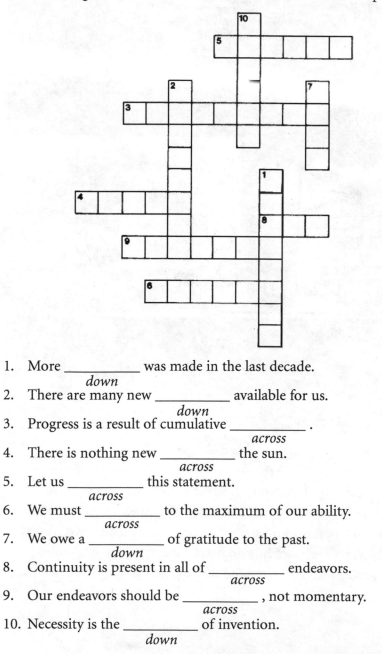

1. More _____ was made in the last decade.
   down
2. There are many new _____ available for us.
   down
3. Progress is a result of cumulative _____ .
   across
4. There is nothing new _____ the sun.
   across
5. Let us _____ this statement.
   across
6. We must _____ to the maximum of our ability.
   across
7. We owe a _____ of gratitude to the past.
   down
8. Continuity is present in all of _____ endeavors.
   across
9. Our endeavors should be _____ , not momentary.
   across
10. Necessity is the _____ of invention.
    down

Song

This song is called *traditional*. It is a railroad worker's song from the days the railroad was being built to transport people from the east of the North American continent to the Pacific coast. First, read the words and learn their meaning. Try to memorize as many words as possible so that you may sing the entire song and understand it.

I've Been Working on the Railroad

Traditional Song

Answer the following questions:

1. Where are the people working?
2. How long is their daily work?
3. Why are they working?
4. What do they hear?
5. Why does the whistle blow?
6. Who is shouting?
7. Who is Dinah?
8. What is someone doing in the kitchen?
9. Where is Dinah?
10. Is this a happy song?

GRAMMAR

Explanation and Examples

When we **report** or **say** what someone has already said, we will usually change the **verb tense** and the **subject pronoun** of the quoted sentence. The verb is placed one tense further in the past. For example, the verb **remember** is changed to **remembered,** etc.

Examples: He said, "There **is** nothing new under the sun." (direct quote)
What did he say?
He said there **was** nothing new under the sun.
(reported speech)

Molly said, "You must go on." (direct quote)
What did Molly say?
She said I had to go on. (reported speech)
Molly told David he had to go on. (reported speech)

Our *dialogues* are all written as **direct statements.** A direct statement means that we indicate **who** the speaker is and then allow the person to make a statement following the colon (:).

Examples: David: That's not true. (direct statement)
David said that was not true. (reported speech)

Molly: You've lost interest in too many things.
(direct statement)
**Molly said David had lost interest in too
many things.** (reported speech)

Dialogues may also be composed in the form of a **direct quote.**
What that means is that we copy the exact words of the speaker within
quotation marks (" ").

Examples: Arthur said, "I'm going home." (direct quote)
Arthur: I'm going home. (direct statement)
What did Arthur say?
He said that he **was** going home. (reported speech)

Abdul said, "I want to go with you." (direct quote)
Abdul: I want to go with you. (direct statement)
What did Abdul say?
He said that he **wanted** to go with Ali. (reported speech)

Molly said, "I'm angry." (direct quote)
Molly: I'm angry. (direct statement)
What did Molly say?
She said that she **was** angry. (reported speech)

David said, "I'm looking for a job." (direct quote)
David: I'm looking for a job. (direct statement)
What did David say?
He said that he **was** looking for a job. (reported speech)

Practice:

Change the **direct quotes** to **reported speech.** Ask the "What" question first. Read the sentences aloud.

Examples: Ahmed said, "I want to see you tomorrow."
            What did he say?
            He said he wanted to see me tomorrow.

            Molly said, "I went shopping yesterday."
            What did Molly say?
            Molly said she had gone shopping yesterday.

Present Tense

1. He said, "I'm glad to know you."

   _____

   _____

2. She said, "I want to go to the movies."

   _____

   _____

3. David said, "That isn't true."

   _____

   _____

4. Henry said, "I'm pleased with my work."

   _____

   _____

5. Sue said, "I can't go out tonight."

   _____

   _____

Past Tense

1. He said, "I went fishing yesterday."

   _____

   _____

2. She said, "I drove too fast."

   _____

   _____

3. Molly said, "I looked for you at school."

   _____

   _____

4. David said, "I was in the library."

   _____

   _____

5. Henry said, "I did it just as you told me to do it."

Present Perfect

1. He said, "I've been to San Francisco."

   _____

   _____

2. She said, "I've made the trip before."

   _____

   _____

3. David said, "I've tried to do it right."

   _____

   _____

4. Henry said, "I've been happy in the U.S.A."

_____

_____

5. Sue said, "I've been lucky so far."

_____

_____

Change the **direct statements** to **indirect statements.** Read the sentences aloud.

Examples: David: I never finish anything. (direct statement)
David said that he never finished anything.
(indirect statement)

Henry: I need money.   (direct statement)
Henry said that he needed money.   (indirect statement)

1. David: I want to study.

_____

2. Molly: You never finish your work.

_____

3. David: I like it here.

_____

4. Molly: I got some money from my parents.

_____

5. David: I haven't heard from Sue.

_____

6. Molly: I'm thinking of writing a letter to James.

_____

7. David: I know why you can't succeed.

_____

8. Molly: I don't understand you.

_____

9. David: You argue too much.

_____

10. Molly: I'll try to improve on my work.

_____

IDEA RECOGNITION

Copy from the model narrative the sentences expressing the following

1. What is unbelievable

_____

2. When progress was made

_____

3. From what point of view we regard progress

_____

4. Why present and future developments are possible

_____

5. Where everything we do or think goes back to

_____

6. What progress is a result of

_____

7. What someone once said

_____

8. What we may conclude about improving conditions

_____

9. Where we pick up

_____

10. To whom human development owes a debt of gratitude

_____

VOCABULARY ENRICHMENT

The following are substitution drills based on the model dialogue presentation. They are to be practiced in pairs. First repeat the drills, then try to compose similar drills with your own words. Repeat the drills aloud.

1. I ask you, **"Have you written**   **your homework?"**
   I asked you if (whether) you
   had written   your homework.
   "Have you done   the exercises?"
   "if (whether) you had done   the exercises.
   "Have you visited   our friends?"
   If (whether) you had visited our friends.
   "Have you gone   fishing?"
   if (whether) you had gone   fishing.

2. David asked Molly, "Do you know   Sara Gochman
   if (whether) she knew   Sara Gochman
   "Do you remember   our trip?"
   if (whether) she remembered their trip.
   "Are you happy   in New York?"
   if (whether) she was happy   in New York.
   "Have you ever gotten   a speeding ticket?"
   if (whether) she had
   ever gotten   a speeding ticket.

3. He asked me, "Are you going   to the show?"
               if (whether) I was going   to the show.
               "Have you done   your homework?"
               if (whether) I had done   my homework.
               "Have you seen   Molly?"
               if (whether) I had seen   Molly.
               "Did you see   her yesterday?"
               if (whether) I had seen   her yesterday.

4. Molly asked me, "Why don't you   finish your work?"
               why I didn't   finish my work.
               "Why haven't you done   the exercises?"
               why I hadn't done   the exercises.
               "Where have you been   last night?"
               where I had been   last night.
               "What were you doing   in class last week?"
               what I had been doing   in class last week.
               "When will you come   to my house?"
               when I would come   to my house.

Lexical Units

Select the word or phrase from the words listed below that best completes each of the sentences. One selection may be used more than once. Read the sentences aloud.

Example: We look for ways to **improve life.**
           People like to live **comfortably.**

unable	debt of gratitude	distance	maximum
left off	conveniences	necessity	back
nothing	lasting		

1. Scientific and technological progress is good. It offers many
   _____ .

2. Present and future developments don't happen by themselves.
   Everything we develop goes _____ to someone or something
   in the past.

3. Progress is a result of cumulative knowledge. There is _____
   new under the sun.

4. Someone may start working on a special task. But he is
   _____ to finish that task.

5. Other people continue the work. But they are only able to progress
   to the _____ of their ability.

6. Some people lay the foundation. Others go a small _____
   further.

7. If we try hard enough, we may succeed in improving conditions.
   This is possible if we pick up where our predecessors _____ .

8. Continuity is present in all endeavors. We owe a _____ to
   the past.

9. Because of continuity our endeavors are _____ .

10. People always think of inventing new things. They do this because
    of _____ .

STEPS IN CREATIVE EXPRESSION

Indicate the type of sentence on the line. Read the sentences aloud.

Example: Sue said, "I got a speeding ticket."   *direct quote*
_____

1. David: I finish things if I'm interested.   _____

2. Sue said, "You always lose interest."   _____

3. He said he wanted to see me tomorrow.   _____

4. Molly: I'm angry. _____

5. She said that she was angry. _____

6. David: "I'm looking for a job." _____

7. He said that he was looking for a job. _____

8. Abdul: I want to go with you. _____

9. He said that he was going home. _____

10. Ytaka said, "I've got to study now." _____

Change the statements as indicated in parentheses.

Example: Ytaka said, "I'm going home." (direct statement)
        Ytaka: I'm going home.

1. He said, "There is nothing new under the sun." (direct statement)

_____

2. Molly: You must go on. (direct quote)

_____

3. Molly said I had to go on. (direct statement)

_____

4. Molly told David he had to go on. (direct quote)

_____

5. Ytaka said that he was going home. (direct statement)

_____

6. Abdul said, "I want to go with you." (reported speech)

_____

7. Molly: I'm driving to L.A. tonight. (direct quote)

_____

8. David said that he was looking for a job. (direct statement)

_____

9. Ahmed said, "I want to see you tomorrow." (reported speech)

_____

10. She said, "I want to go to the movies." (direct statement)

_____

Change the **direct commands** to **reported speech.**

Example: Molly said to David, "You must go on."
  Molly told David to go on.

1. Sue said to Robert, "Don't drive too fast."

_____

2. Abdul said to Jason, "Don't be late for school."

_____

3. Mrs. Garza said to Joan, "Buy some tomatoes before it's too late."

_____

4. Molly said to David, "Don't say that."

_____

5. The judge said to Sue, "You should slow down in town."

_____

6. Jason said to Robert, "Remember to return the ball."

_____

7. The teacher said to Ali, "Please repeat your question."

_____

8. Ali said to the teacher, "Would you speak slowly?"

_____

9. David said to the waitress, "Would you bring me some coffee?"

_____

10. The waitress said to David, "Will you have anything else?"

_____

Create a dialogue similar to the model presentation, based on the expressions below. Read the dialogue aloud. (Marcel = M, Hiromi = H)

M: Why does _____ tell me? "You _____ go on!"

H: _____ they know _____ too many things _____ .

M: _____ not true.

H: _____ you mean?

M: _____ start something _____ finish _____ if interested.

H: _____ lose interest?

M: _____ give _____ up.

H: You _____ continue _____ work.

M: I'll remember _____ and I'll _____ to improve .

COMMENTARY ON MODEL PRESENTATION

Using key words and phrases from the model narrative, comment on the topics presented below.

invention	development	distance further
unbelievable	work done in the past	improve
progress	nothing new	predecessors
decade	ponder	debt of gratitude
century	carefully	continuity
regard	task	lasting
not momentary	point of view	maximum ability
endeavor	issue	laid the foundation
necessity	conveniences	

1. a. Comment on what you think about inventing.
    b. Tell about an inventor you know.
    c. Give your views about technological and scientific progress.
    d. Tell what you think about continuity.
    e. Talk about our debt to our ancestors.

2. a. Discuss the points in the model narrative with which you agree.
    b. Mention the points in the model narrative that you think are possible to accomplish.
    c. Talk about the points in the model narrative with which you disagree.
    d. Give an appropriate title to your composition.

FREE COMPOSITION

Dialogue Improvisation

Compose your own dialogue using the situation given below. Repeat the dialogue aloud.

1. You are disappointed about your last test.
2. Your friend thinks you didn't study enough.
3. You think the test wasn't fair.
4. Your friend wants to go to the movies.
5. You are getting angry with your friend.
6. Your friend tries to convince you not to worry.
7. You don't want to continue the conversation.
8. Your friend asks you to call him.
9. You promise to call that evening.
10. Both of you say your good-byes.

Fill in the Missing Dialogue

For each of the drawings below, write your own dialogue which describes the action.

Compose a short narrative, building on the expressions given below.

1. . . . almost unbelievable . . . scientific and technological progress this seems to be true . . . point of view . . . household. . .

2. what we must always remember . . . present and future . . . in the past. Progress is. . . cumulative . . . someone said . . .

3. if we ponder. . . carefully . . . conclude . . . started the task . . . unable to finish . . . continued and progressed . . . the foundation . . . laid. . . small distance . . . others . . . improve . . . the future.

4. thus . . . predecessors left off . . .all human . . . a debt of gratitude . . . to the past . . . continuity is . . . all endeavor. . . lasting . . . momentary . . . and in all . . . repeat quite honestly . . . adage "Necessity is. . . ."

Active Vocabulary

Words are listed in alphabetical order. All main entries appear in italics; their synonyms or definitions are set in roman type. The number and letter following each entry indicate the chapter (1-10), model presentation (D = dialogue, N = narrative), vignette (V), or song (S) where the word was used, i.e., *age*-time 8N = chapter 8, narrative.

a couple–a few	4D	*advantage*–benefit	1N
about to–ready to, prepared to	3V	*adviser*–consultant	6N
abstain from–stay away from	2D	*afford*–bear	1N
accept–take, receive	8N	*age*–time	8N
accident–unfortunate event resulting from carelessness; mishap	6D	*ahead of*–before, in front of	3N
		all for–completely in favor of or in agreement with	3N
accomplishments–skills, achievements	5N	*all over*–everywhere	4D
according to–as stated by, on the authority of	3D	*allergic*–have a bad reaction to	3D
		allow–permit	2N
account for–explain	2D	*along with*–in addition to, together with	3D
ache–pain, hurt	2D	*amazed*–surprised, astonished	5S
achieve–accomplish	5N	*ambitious*–wanting more wealth	6N
acted–done	8N		
adage–proverb, saying	10N	*ancestors*–forefathers	6N
admires–likes	1N	*ancient*–of times long past, old	6N
admission–confession	6D		
admit–acknowledge	10D	*answer*–solution	8D

anticipate–look forward to   1S

anxious–eager   4D

apart from–besides,
   separate from   3D

approximately–more or less   4V

area–place, locality   4V

argue with–disagree with,
   be contrary with   2D

arid–dry, nonproductive   8N

as for–referring to
   (something)   3D

ask about–inquire   2D

ask for–request   2D

assume–suppose   7N

at first–originally,
   in the beginning   3N

at last–finally   3N

at the time of–during, while   3D

at this very moment–
   right now   7D

atmosphere–feeling, spirit   8V

attempted–tried   2V

attentively–thoughtfully
   paying attention   7D

attracted–captivated   9V

attribu te–quality   8N

avoid–keep away from   3N

background–origin   3N

balcony–small platform
   rojecting from a wall
   of a building   6N

ball–formal dance   8V

balmy–mild   5S

band–orchestra   8V

bankroll–fortune, supply
   of money   9N

base–foundation, support   6V

basic–fundamental   5N

be aware recognize   2N

be better off–(idiom) have
   an advantage   3D

because of–on account of   3D

become of–happen to   1N

beginning–inception   5N

belief–faith   8N

betray–reveal, show   4V

beware of–be watchful   2N

bite one's head off–answer
   in anger   4N

blame for–hold responsible
   for, condemn   2D

blindly–without question   5N

bloodshed–killing   6N

blooming–blossoming   9S

blow over–subside, become
   less serious   4N

blow up–explode   8N

bottom–lowest point   7V

bound for–going to   3N

bound to–likely to   3N

brand–trademark   3D

break even–gain or lose
   nothing in a transaction   4N

break in –burglarize, rob   7N

breathe–inhale   2N

bright–shining with light   5S

bring along–include in one's

company, accompany 4D

bring back–return, recall ID

bring up–mention ID

build–create, make 4V

busy–preoccupied 5D

buy–purchase 9N

buy up–to buy all that
is available 3D

by ear–without reading music 3N

by way of–via 3N

call up–telephone ID

cancellation–change of
appointment date 2D

canyon–narrow valley
between high cliffs 7V

carefully–cautiously 10N

carnival–festival, exhibition 8V

carriage–coach, vehicle 4N

cause–reason 8N, 9N

caution against–warn 2D

cavity–hole 2D

century–one hundred years 4V, 10N

changed–altered 5N

cheer up–be glad, happy 1N

choice–option 2D

chose, chosen–selected 8V, 9N

closely knit–intimate 9D

coast–seashore 4V

coaxed–persuaded 9V

combine–put together 1N

come across–meet by chance 1N

come along–accompany 1D

come over–pay a visit 1D

common–usual, everday thing 3D

commonplace–everyday thing 5D

compare–liken 9N

competitive–based on rivalry 9N

complain about–express
discontent with, fret 2D

completed–finished 9D

complication–involved or
confused condition 3D

concentrate–pay attention 5D

concerned–involved 3N

conditioning–exercising,
getting fit 1N

confidence–belief, trust,
assurance 5N, 8N

confrontation–face-to-face
challenge 6N

consider–keep in mind 6D

consume–eat 1N

contain–consist of, hold 2D

contents–things inside, amount
contained 6D

continent–part of the globe
(earth) 4N

continuity–uninterrupted
succession, uniformity 10N

contribute to–be responsible
for, give 2N, 5N

control–dominate 9N

convenience–comforts, useful
things conducive to comfort
8N, 10N

corruption–dishonesty 5N

costly–expensive 6D

count on–depend on,
rely on 1D, 2D

countless–too many
    to count 8V
courage–bravery, valor 7D, 10D
courtesy–politeness 3D
courtin' (courting)–trying
    to enamor 8S
covering–traveling 4N
crops–food grown to sell 2V
cross–go from one to the
    other side, traverse 4N
cross-ties–beams or posts
    placed under the rails
    crosswise for support 8S
cruelty–brutality 8N
cumulative–progressive
    addition 7D
curlew–large wading bird 5S
customer–client, consumer 3D
customs–immigration
    procedures 4D

damage–injury, loss of value 6D
daydream–have pleasant
    thoughts 6D
deal in–sell, do business in,
    be engaged in 4N
debt–obligation 10N
decade–ten years 10N
decided–determined 6N
decline–aging 1N
deeds–actions 5N
deep–profound, intelligent 8D
delay–slowdown 9D
delivered–brought 9D
demand–want, ask for 6N

depend on–rely on,
    count on 2N, 7N
designed–planned
determine–find out,
    discover 7D
development–growth 10N
dictated–forced
diet–eat special food 1N
differ–be different, vary,
    disagree with 4N
difference–dissimilarity 7D
different–not alike, distinct 7D
dignity–worth, merit 8N
disagree with–be contrary
    with, argue with 2D
disappear–vanish 6N
discipline–skill 1N
discouraging–negative 5N
displayed–shown 9N
distance–expanse, space
    between two points;
    course; extent 4N, 9V, 10N
distinguish–show a
    difference, differentiate 3N
diversity–difference, variety 4V
do about (it)–correct (it) 10D
donated–given 9D
down and out–without
    money, destitute 3N
draw interest–earn money
    on capital 4N
dream house–ideal home 9N
drink up–finish a drink
    completely 4N
drove–led, moved 2V
dumb–stupid 5D

earning–money making 9N

eat out–eat in a restaurant 4N

ecstasy–feeling of great joy 4N

effective–active 3N

effort–attempt 2N

elect–choose 8N

element–substance, material 2N

elsewhere–somewhere else 9V

endeavor–work 10N

entertaining–amusing 8V

entire–whole 1N, 3N, 6N

environment–surroundings 2N

envy–be jealous of,
    begrudge 8D, 9D

equally–alike, the same
    way, evenly 8N

establish–settle, institute 5N

event–happening 9 V

evil–wrong, bad 5N, 6N

exactly–correctly, precisely 3D, 10D

examine–study 7D

exceed–go beyond, be
    greater than 5S, 6D

except for–with the
    exception of 3D

exciting–thrilling, wonderful 8D

experience–personal
    involvement 7D

explore–search, investigate 7D

explosion–blowup 6N

explosive–something that
    can explode 8N

facts–things 9N

failure– lack of success 4N

fall apart–be destroyed 3N

fall in love with–
    become enamored of 2N

false–untrue 8S

fancy–extravagant 7N

fantasy–imagination 7D

fashion–make, shape 4N

fasten–attach 4N

fault–weakness 10D

favorably–advantageously 9N

feasting–eating well 8V

fertile–fruitful 8N

festivity–celebration 2V

figure out–reason, solve
    the problem 1D

fine–penalty 5D

finish –accomplish 10D

fitness–good health 1N

flexibility–elasticity, agility 1N

flickering–burning unsteadily,
    as a candle in the wind 5S

flight–trip (by jet or airplane) 4D

float–parade exhibit
    mounted on a vehicle 8V

flocks–groups of animals 5S

flow–progress 5N

folks–people 9D

foolish–silly 8D

for ever and ever–always 3N

for keeps–the real or actual

for lack of–in place of 3D

for once–one time 6N

for the time being–temporarily,
    for now 3N

force of gravity–force drawing

all bodies toward the
center of the earth 4N

foresee–know ahead of time,
imagine 5N

form–create 7V

foundation–base 7V, 10N

free from–without 5N

frequent–visit 9N

from time to time–
occasionally, not often,
now and then 3N

gain–win 8N

game–entertainment 9N

gathering–party 9N

gazed–stared 5S

generally–usually 7N

geology–earth science 7V

gestures–body movements 3N

get off–leave any means
of transporation 4N

get rid of–discard, lose
intentionally 3D

get up–wake up 1D

gift–natural ability, present 3N, 6V

give a ring–call up, telephone 4D

give in–yield, surrender 6N

give up–surrender,
quit, stop 1D, 10D

gliding–sliding 5S

glittering–sparkling, shining 5S

globe–earth 4N

glory–great honor, value 5S

go about–act, proceed 1N

go easy on–don't be angry with 5D

go on–happen, continue 1D, 10D

gone–away 7N

gossip–talk in a chatty way
about others 9N

govern–guide 6N

graceful–having beauty;
moving easily 5S

grant–give 7N

gratitude–thankfulness,
thanks 7N, 10N

graze–eat grass 5S

grown man–adult, grownup 5D

guarantee–ensure 7N

guard against–be watchful,
foresee and prevent 2N

guilt–fault, error 6D

had it coming–expected it 8D

hardship –difficulty 4N

harm–damage, destruction 2N

harmful–hurt 2D

harmony–peace, agreement 4N

head on– continue 3V

hear of–know about (the
existence of) someone
or something 2D

heel–terrible person 8D

highest priority–of greatest
importance 3N

hire–to employ 2V

holds–keeps 8D

honest–true 10D

how's that?–what are
you saying? 6D

hug–embrace 8S

huge–very big 4N

human nature–the way people are 7N

hunger–have no food 6N

hurl–throw or fling with force 4N

ignorance–lack of knowledge 5N

ignorant–uneducated 6N

I'll be–(expression of surprise) 5D

imagine–visualize 7D

impress–affect, have an impact on 8N

improve–better, make progress, make better 2N

improvement–getting better 8D

in addition to–besides 3N

in behalf of–speaking (acting) for 3D

in between–in the area (time) between 3D

in case of–in the event of 3D

in comparison to (with)– compared with 3N

in contrast to–as opposed to, different from 3N

in front of–located before 3D

in place of–as a substitute or replacement for 3D

in search of–looking for 3D

in spite of–notwithstanding; disregarding the difficulty or resistance, contrary to 2N, 3D

in the face of–when confronted with 3N

in the first place–initially 8D

in time–within the required time, not late 3N

in tune with–in agreement or accord with 3N

in vain–without any result, futile 3N

inaugurated–started 9V

increasing–rising 9N

incurable–fatal 1N

inevitable–unavoidable 1N

infinite–endless 4N

influence–have an effect upon 5N

inhabit–live in 4V, 7D

instead of–in place of 8N

intend to–mean to 2N

interest–profit 1D

interested–curious 10D

interrupt–break in on someone's talk 6D

invention–discovery, finding 4N

inventor–one who creates things 4N

issue–topic, matter 2N, 10N

jar–container 3D

jogging–running 1N

keep an eye on–spy 9N

keep on–continue 1D, 1N

king–monarch 6N

label–description of the drug 3D

lack–need, absence, want 4N, 8N

lasting–enduring 10N

latest–news 5D

layer–single thickness lying over or under another 7V

leader–one who governs, guides 6N

laft off–stopped 10N

leisurely–slowly 5S

level–condition, degree 3N

liberate–free 8N

liberty–freedom 6V

limit–end 7D

limited–restricted, narrow 4N

local anesthetic–drug to reduce pain or feeling 2D

loneliness–sadness from being alone, desolation, solitariness 2V

look at–inspect 2D

look forward to–anticipate 1N

look like–seem 2D

look out for–be careful about 1D

look over–examine 1D

magic–charm 9V

maintain–keep up, continue, keep 1N, 2N

make it–attend, be present at 4D

make the best of–try to succeed 9D

make up–invent 2V

make up (mind)–decide 1N

market–place to buy and sell 2V

marketplace–where things are sold 6N

material–physical 7N, 9N

materialistic–based on things, matter, wanting more material goods 1N

matter–thing, subject 5D

matter of factly–truthfully 3N

maximum–best, greatest, highest 10N

means–way, ability 2N,3N

measure–degree 1N

mechanized–automated 2N

melt–dissolve 4N

Memorial Day–U.S. legal holiday commemorating dead servicemen 9V

merchandise–things to sell and buy 3D

mid-nineteenth century– circa 1850 2V

miracle–supernatural thing or event 3D

mislead–deceived 5N

miss–feel the absence of 9D

misunderstanding– disagreement, misinterpretation 3N

misuse–abuse, use badly 2N

moderate–cautious, careful 1N

molar–tooth in the back of the mouth 2D

momentary–temporary 10N

motorist–driver 6D

nearby–close to here 4D

newcomers–recent arrivals 4V

news media–radio,
   newspapers, etc.   7N
no longer–no more   6N
nodding–moving the head
   up and down   3N
none of–no more   6N
nonpredatory–not living on
   other animals   8N
nourishment–food   1N

obey–follow commands   6D
obstacle–hindrance, difficulty   4N
of age–eighteen years or older   3N
office–service   8N
official–authorized   4V
often–frequently   9N
oftentimes–many times   7N
ointment–substance, salve   3D
on account of –due to   3D
on and on–continuously,
   always   6N
on the whole–all things
   considered, generally   4D
opinion–point of view,
   belief, view, conviction   3N, 8D
opportunity–chance   4N
ordinarily–usually   2D
organized–instituted   9D
out of–out of stock,
   unavailable   3D
out of date–obsolete, no
   longer in fashion   3N
out of order–not working
   properly, broken   3N
outfit–suit, dress   1D

outlet–activity   1N
overweight–too heavy   1N

palace–castle, large
   fortified building   6N
parade–a marching show   8V
partin' (parting)–separating
pass by–go by, past   2V
pastime–recreation   9N
patience–calmness,
   forbearance   3D
pay attention–be careful
   look out for, listen   5D, 6D
pay back–repay   1D
pay for–repay   1D
perfect–without defect   4N
period–time   1N
personal–individual   10D
pick out–select   1D
pick up–fetch, start   1D, 10N
pippin' (pipping)–still inside
   the egg   9S
planet–celestial body   7D
plans–designs   9D
point–show, aim   8N
ponder–consider, think deeply   10N
popular–common, what
   people like   1N,6V
possessions–belongings   7N,9N
posted–announced   5D
pouring–flowing   1N
poverty–need   6N
powerful–strong, mighty   6N
practice–do something
   repeatedly   3N

precious–valuable 2N

predecessors–ancestors 10N

prepare–arrange, make ready 7D

pressed from–driven from,
exiled 5S

presume–think 2D

pretty–quite 7N

pride–conceit, exaggerated
opinion of oneself 6N

primitive–simple 8N

prior to–before 2V

probably–likely 7N

problem–difficulty,
unsettled question 5N, 8D

process–steps, system 1N, 7D

progress–improvement 10N

proper–suitable, specific 3N

prosperous–rich,
well-to-do 7N

protection–safety 2V

provided–if 7D

providing–affording, giving 1N

pumping–pulsating 1N

pure–clean 2N

purpose–goal, aim, plan 4V

pursue–engage in, practice 4N

put off–postpone 1N

put on–get dressed 1D

put up–offered 9D

quest–desire 5N

race–contest, competition 9V

rain check–another chance 5D

raising–breeding, growing 2 V

rancher–farmer who
raises cattle 2V

reach –arrive at 3 V

reality–real, fact 4N

rebel–resist 6N

rebirth–born again 8N

receptionist–one who
receives patients and
gives information 2D

recorded–set down in writing 8N

reduce–lose weight 1N

refer to–call 2N

refrain from–abstain from 2D

regarded–thought of,
considered, looked at 9N, 10N

regardless of–no matter,
irrespective of 3D, 3N

regularly–usually 1N

reign–rule 8 V

relating to–applying to 3N

relative to–concerning,
related to 3N

relieve–ease, reduce 3D

religious–relating to religion 8N

rely on–depend on, count on 2N

remain–stay 2N, 7N

remote–distant, far away 7V

renovated–renewed, remodeled 9D

repeat–do again 8N

repeatedly–again and again 6N

reply–answer 7N

requires–needs 1N

reservation–a place reserved
or assigned 4V

reside–live 3V

resources–raw materials 4N

result from–be a
   consequence of 2D

right on–continued 6N

rim–edge 7 V

robbery–hold up, theft 5D

rodeo–a cowboy contest of skill 2V

rolling–turning over and over 9S

romantic –sentimental 2V

round up–collection of cattle
   into one place 2V

ruby-colored–red 7 V

rule–govern, dictate 6N

ruler–monaich, leader,
   dictator 4V, 6N

rural–country 9D

safe–secure 7N

satisfied–contented 7N

scenery–view 7V

scream–yell 5S

season–time 8 V

seat of government–place where
   government is carried on 3V

second best–not the very best 8D

secret–something kept
   hidden to oneself 5D

seek–look for 4V

select–choose 7D

self-deceit–dishonesty
   with oneself 3N

self-esteem– self-respect 5N

self-gratification–
   self-satisfaction 9N

settle–establish residence 4V

share–part, portion 2N

side by side–next to one
   another as neighbors 4V

sight–something to
   see, view 6V, 7V

silence–quiet 6N

silly–foolish 8D

skinny–thin, lean 1N

smart–wise 7D

so long–farewell, good-bye ID, 4D

social–friendly; relating
   to the interaction of
   human beings 9N

solar system–the sun and all
   the heavenly bodies 7D

solving–resolving 5N

sooner or later–eventually 1N

sophisticated–refined 3N

speak out–express oneself
   courageously and freely 4N

speed–velocity 5D, 6D

speed trap–check point for
   speeding drivers 5D

stand–bear 4V

stand for–mean, signify 6V

start–begin 10D

statue–sculpture, work of art 6V

status symbols–things that
   suggest wealth 9N

steal–take illegally 2V

steam–boiling water turned
   into vapor 4N

strange–unusual 7D

stream–body of running water 7V

strength–power 1N

stretching–muscle expansion 1N
strike–protest 9D
subject–topic 7D
subjects–people under the
    authority or control of
    a ruler 6N
sufficient–enough 1N
suggest–hint 5D
suitable–appropriate 3D
supposing–imagining 7N
surround–encircle 2N
survive–go on living 2N
sustained–long lasting 1N
sympathize–feel for (someone),
    commiserate with 2D

take for granted–accept
    as true 5N
take off–remove, shed 1N
take on–try to do, undertake 1N
take over–to manage, rule 6N
take the trouble–make an
    effort, try 5N
take up–become involved with 1N
take up time–consume time 4N
takes in–is comprised of 3V
talk over–discuss ID
temporarily–briefly, for a
    limited time 3D
term of office–duration of
    a position 3V
territory–land 4 V
theme–topic 8V
they'd–they would 5D
thrilled–excited 9D

throne–royal chair 6N
throughout–all through 7N
throw up–get rid of ID
counter–place where tickets
    are sold 4D
tiny–very small 6N
tolerance–acceptance of
    differences in beliefs
    or customs 4N
torch–a burning light 6V
tough–very hard, difficult 4D
traffic sign–road signal 6D
traffic ticket–summons
    for driving too fast 5D
tragedy–misfortune 4V
trap–ambush, catch 6D
treated–cared for 9D
true–faithful 7D
trusted–faithful 1N
try on–test, examine ID
turn around–look (back) 8D
turn off–make a turn ID
turn over–transfer ID
tyranny–cruel rule 4V, 6N

unbelievable–unthinkable 1 ON
unique –peculiar, unusual;
    unequaled 3N
unity–togetherness 4V
universally–generally, all over 1N
unpretentious–simple 7N
unsafe–not safe 2N
up and about–able to move
    about (after an illness) 3V
up to date– modern, current 3V

upside down–inverted;
   disarranged, in confusion   3V
used to be–was   4V
useful–helpful, productive   3N
value–worth, esteem   8N
varied–different   3N
vigor–energy, vitality   1N
vocalization–speech, voice   3N

wage–carry on   8N
wait for–defay, expect   2D
waiting (my) turn–
   standing in line   4D
walk of life–activity   4V
warm up–*to* get warm   1D
warn–give notice   6D
waterfall–falling water   7V
wax–substance used for
   making candles   4N
ways–customs, how a
   person behaves   6N
weakened–softened   9N

wealth–riches, affluence   9N
wealthy–rich   7N
welcome–greet   6V
what's up–what is happening   4D
willing–wanting   8N
winding–curvy   9V
wisdom– intelligence,
   good judgment   7N
wish for–want   2N
with respect to–concerning,
   with regard to   3D
with the intention of–
   intending to   3D
wonder–be curious   6N
work up–create; prepare
   a solution or answer;
   advance   1D,2V
worry–distress   9N
worth– value   5N

zephyr–soft wind   5S
zone–section, area   6D

Appendix I

Two-Word Verbs

When a verb and preposition are used together, they have a single meaning different from that of the two words when used seperately. Even though two-word verbs are often used in the English language they are not included in commonly used dictionaries, and their idiomatic meanings must be learned in context.

Verb–intransitive

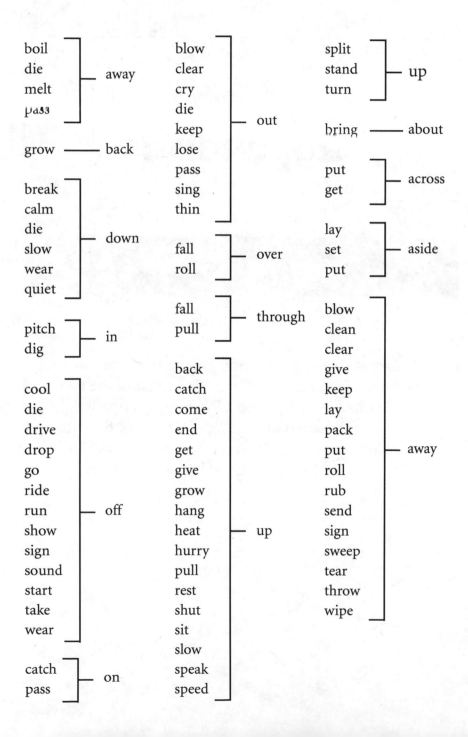

boil, die, melt, pass	away
grow	back
break, calm, die, slow, wear, quiet	down
pitch, dig	in
cool, die, drive, drop, go, ride, run, show, sign, sound, start, take, wear	off
catch, pass	on
blow, clear, cry, die, keep, lose, pass, sing, thin	out
fall, roll	over
fall, pull	through
back, catch, come, end, get, give, grow, hang, heat, hurry, pull, rest, shut, sit, slow, speak, speed	up
split, stand, turn	up
bring	about
put, get	across
lay, set, put	aside
blow, clean, clear, give, keep, lay, pack, put, roll, rub, send, sign, sweep, tear, throw, wipe	away

cut	rub	even
drive	run	fence
feed	set	fight
hold	shoot	finish
keep	shut	head
play — back	take	hold
read	tear — down	laugh
set	throw	let
take	turn	make
turn	vote	pass
win	wash	pay
	wear	pull
pass — by	write	rinse
		rope
beat	put — forth	round
break	set	rub
bring		run — off
burn	bring	send
chop	cash — in	set
count	push	shake
drink	take	shave
fasten		shoot
flag	beat	show
force	block	shut
hand — down	break	sweep
hunt	bring	take
jot	brush	tell
keep	buy	throw
lay	call	tip
let	carry — off	top
mark	check	touch
narrow	clear	ward
note	clip	wash
pin	cut	write
play	dash	
put	cry	

act		round		blow	
blow		rule		build	
bring		send		burn	
call		set		call	
carry		sort		cheer	
clean		spread		cover	
cross		stamp		dig	
crowd		straighten	— out	drink	
cut		stretch		eat	
dig		take		fill	
drown		thin		finish	
dry		throw		give	
empty		tire		heat	
even		turn		hold	
figure		wash		keep	
fill	— out	wear		lock	
find		work		look	
give				mix	
hand		check		move	
help		do		open	
hold		hold		pack	
keep		look		pick	
lay		pass		roll	
let		put		save	— up
measure		read	— over	shake	
move		run		sign	
pick		take		sum	
point		talk		think	
pour		think		tighten	
pull				use	
rip		put	— through	wake	
		see		wrap	

Appendix II

Compound Prepositions

Two or more words are frequently used as single prepositions. These compound prepositions are very common in English, particularly written English. Compound prepositions are frequently idiomatic and need to be learned in context.

according to—as stated by, on the authority of

ahead of—before, in front of

along with—together with, concurrently with

alongside of— beside, parallel with

apart from—separate from, considered in separation from, aside from, away from

as against—in contrast or competition with, as opposed to

as between—choosing or judging between two

as compared with (to)—in comparison with

as for—(used to introduce a new but similar subject for consideration or comment), but for, except for, save for

at the cost of— costing

at the hands of— by someone

at the point of— about to do something . . . followed by a noun or gerund

at the risk of—risking

at the time of— during the time (something else happened)

because of—on account of

by dint of—because

by force of—by the power of

by means of—through the use or agency of

by order of—on orders from

by reason of—because, on account of

by virtue of—by the authority or prestige of

by way of—via

due to—on account of

except for—with the exception of

for fear of—because of fear of

for lack of—because of not having

for the purpose of— in order to . . . followed by gerund

for the sake of—in the interests of, for the good of

from above—from a position above or over

from behind—from a position behind

from over—from the direction of

in accordance with—in agreement with

in addition to—added to, besides

in behalf of—speaking or acting as a proxy or representative of

in between—in the area or time between

in care of—in the custody of

in case of—in the event of

in close connection with—in cooperation with

in common with—sharing the same nature or behavior as

in comparison to (or with)—compared with

in compliance with—yielding or submitting to

in connection with—as an aspect or consequence of

in consequence of—taking into account, considering

in contrast to (with)— as opposed to

in deference to—submitting to the attitudes, opinions, or wishes of

in exchange for—in return for

in front of—located before

in lieu of—as a substitute for, in place of

in opposition to—opposing

in place of—as a substitute or replacement for

in preference to—being preferred to

in regard to—concerning

in search of—looking for

in spite of—notwithstanding, disregarding the difficulty or resistance of

in terms of—from the aspect of

in the course of—during

in the event of—in case of

in the face of—in the presence of

independently of—without dependence on

inside of—within (refers to either place or time)

instead of—in place of, substituting for

on account of—because of

on behalf of—speaking or acting as a proxy or representative of

on top of— on the highest surface of; furthermore, in addition

out of—from the interior of; no longer in or within (as in the idioms
       out of sight, out of mind, etc.)

outside of—beyond the limits of an area; with the exception of

owing to—because of

previous to—before a certain time
regardless of—without regarding, irrespective of
relating to—having some relation with
relative to—concerning
round about (around about)—at approximately (. . . usually said of time)
short of—with the ultimate exception of
under cover of— concealed by, protected by
with a view to—for the purpose of, intending to
with reference to—referring to *with* for *in)*
with regard to—with respect to, concerning
with respect to—in regard to, concerning
with the intention of— intending to

Appendix III

The Principal Parts
of Irregular Verbs

A complete list of *irregular* verbs and their principal
parts may be found in every good dictionary.
Included here for the convenience of the
reader are some more commonly used
irregular verbs and their principal parts.

The first principal part of a verb is the *infinitive* (simple form of the verb); the second principal part is the *past tense*; and the third principal part is the *past participle*. We don't ordinarily consider the *present participle* to be one of the principal parts because it is always regular and is quite simple to construct, i.e., be-being, go-going, have-having, do—doing, etc.

Infinitive	*Past Tense*	*Past Participle*
awake	awaked, awoke	awaked, awaken
be	was	were, been
become	became	become
begin	began	begun
bite	bit	bitten
bleed	bled	bled
blow	blew	blown
break	broke	broken
bring	brought	brought
build	built	built
buy	bought	bought
catch	caught	caught
choose	chose	chosen
come	came	come
deal	dealt	dealt
dig	dug	dug
dive	dived, dove	dived
do	did	done
draw	drew	drawn
dream	dreamt, dreamed	dreamt, dreamed
drink	drank	drunk*
drive	drove	driven
eat	ate	eaten
fall	fell	fallen
feel	felt	felt

---

* We form adjectives of some of these past/participles by adding *en*, i.e., drunken person, sunken treasure, etc.

fight	fought	fought
find	found	found
fly	flew	flown
forbid	forbad(e)	forbidden
forget	forgot	forgot, forgotten
forgive	forgave	forgiven
freeze	froze	frozen
get	got	got, gotten
give	gave	given
go	went	gone
grow	grew	grown
hang	hung, hanged	hung, hanged
have	had	had
hear	heard	heard
hide	hid	hidden
hold	held	held
keep	kept	kept
know	knew	known
lay	laid	laid
leave	left	left
lie (recline)	lay	lain
lie (tell a lie)	lied	lied
lose	lost	lost
make	made	made
meet	met	met
overdraw	overdrew	overdrawn
pay	paid	paid
read	read	read
ride	rode	ridden
ring	rang	rung
run	ran	run
say	said	said
see	saw	seen
sell	sold	sold
send	sent	sent

shake	shook	shaken
shoot	shot	shot
show	showed	shown
shrink	shrank	shrunk
sing	sang	sung
sink	sank	sunk
sit	sat	sat
sleep	slept	slept
speak	spoke	spoken
speed	sped	sped
spend	spent	spent
stand	stood	stood
steal	stole	stolen
stink	stank	stunk
strive	strove	stiven
swear	swore	sworn
swim	swam	swum
take	took	taken
teach	taught	taught
tear	tore	torn
tell	told	told
think	thought	thought
throw	threw	thrown
understand	understood	understood
wake	waked, woke	woke
wear	wore	worn
weave	wove	woven
win	won	won
wind	wound	wound
withdraw	withdrew	withdrawn
write	wrote	written

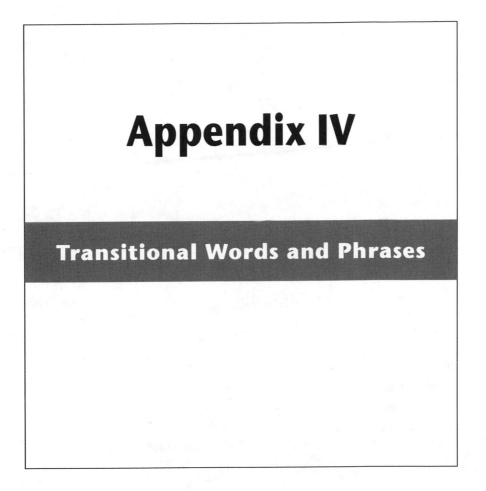

Appendix IV

Transitional Words and Phrases

CHRONOLOGICAL

after*	later
after(ward(s))	meanwhile
as*	next
at that time	now
before*	soon
during**	then
eventually	until*
finally	when(ever)
first, second, etc.	while
in the meantime	

ANALYTICAL AND COMPARATIVE

also	in addition (to)
and	in this case
another	likewise
finally	moreover
first, second, etc.	next
for instance	provided (that)
furthermore	then

RELATING TO SPACE

above	in front of
across from	near (by)
around	next to
behind	on the left
below	on the right
beneath	on top of

---

* Subordinating conjunctions.

** Prepositions and comparatives that cannot introduce a complete thought.

beyond
close to
down
further
here

over
there
under (neath)
up

SHOWING CONTRAST

(al)though*
before . . . after
but
despite**
different from**
earlier. . . later
even though*
however
in spite of**
less than**
more than**
nevertheless
not only . . . but also**

on the other hand
some . . . others
the former . . . the latter
then . . . now
this . . . that
unless*
unlike**
whereas*
while*
years ago . . . today
yet

CONCLUSION

as a result (of)
at last
because (of)*
consequently
finally
for this reason . . . those reasons
if*

in closing
in conclusion
in summary
since*
so that*
therefore
thus

Index